RUGBY LEAGUE

JOURNAL

ANNUAL
2005

RUGBY LEAGUE JOURNAL

PUBLISHING

First published in Great Britain in 2004 by
Rugby League Journal Publishing
P.O.Box 22, Egremont, Cumbria, CA23 3WA

ISBN 0-9548355-0-6

Edited and designed by Harry Edgar

Sales and Marketing by Ruth Edgar

FRONT COVER PICTURE: The infamous "Watersplash" Wembley Final of 1968 as Wakefield Trinity's Don Fox hits the turf tackled by Mick Shoebottom of Leeds.

RUGBY LEAGUE JOURNAL
PUBLISHING

P.O. Box 22, Egremont, Cumbria, CA23 3WA
E-Mail: rugbyleague.journal@virgin.net   Telephone: 01946 814249
www.rugbyleaguejournal.com

CONTENTS

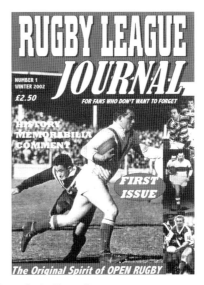

For details of
Rugby League Journal
BACK-ISSUES - Page 101
SUBSCRIPTIONS - Page 82

(Above) Jimmy Ledgard, one of Great Britain's heroes of the inagural World Cup competition played 50 years ago in the autumn of 1954, pictured in Britain's very first World Cup game which was against Australia in the Stade de Gerland in Lyon on 31st October 1954.

(Right) Roger Millward, the little maestro who played such a key role in Great Britain's last winning of the Ashes, pictured in the third and deciding Test of that series played on 4th July 1970 at the Sydney Cricket Ground.

This book is dedicated to the game we used to know and to all the men like Jimmy Ledgard and Roger Millward who shaped the great events of its wonderful history.

Introduction

NOSTALGIA MAN
symbol of the
"Rugby League Journal"

If you have never seen a copy of the quarterly publication *"Rugby League Journal,"* you might be wondering what this Annual is all about. A book that mixes stacks of nostalgia, memorabilia, old photographs and memories of years gone by in Rugby League, with comment and analysis on the present day game.

That is the mixture that has made the quarterly *"Journal"* such a popular success with fans who don't want to forget the game they used to know - and we hope this first *"Rugby League Journal Annual"* will provide a bumper package of enjoyment for all followers of the game, especially those with long memories.

The mixture of old and new in Rugby League is always fascinating and can turn up some very stark contrasts. And the aim of every issue of the *"Journal"* - just as it is with this Annual - is two-fold. Firstly, to help rekindle memories for older fans of the players, teams and events they knew in their youth; secondly, to help educate the younger generation of supporters about the great history of Rugby League and the many fine people who shaped it. In addition, the *"Journal"* has comment and analysis on current events in the world of Rugby League by very experienced writers who have been involved in the game for many years.

The Rugby League we see today is very different to the game many of us were brought up with. Many of the changes have been for the better, some have not, but the game at its best remains a tremendous spectacle which demands the highest levels of fitness, skill, intelligence, toughness and courage from its players. Rugby League has a great history of being an innovator which has led the way for other sports to follow. Yet those of us who produce the *"Journal"* bemoan the loss of many aspects of the game we used to know...

Joe Egan, one of the great British internationals who we believe should all be recognised and honoured as we present the full register of Great Britain players. Joe is pictured (above) in the days when Test caps were awarded.

from Lions tours, Kangaroo tours and Boxing Day derbies to competitive scrums and ball-handling props like Arthur Beetson, Terry Clawson or Brian McTigue.

We have always been in the vanguard for promoting Rugby League with colour, style and an expansive approach to developing the game accross all geographical and social boundaries. But now we come from an old school who wince with embarrassment at such famous institutions as Wakefield Trinity or Wigan being referred to as the "Wildcats" or the "Warriors."

If you share our view that Rugby League was much more interesting in the days when a whole host of clubs felt they were part of the mainstream - including such teams as Barrow, Dewsbury, Featherstone Rovers, Halifax, Oldham, Hull Kingston Rovers, Leigh, Hunslet, Swinton, Workington Town or York - and not just an elite four or five dominated things, then you'll know that the *"Rugby League Journal"* is for you.

This Annual presents a mixture of records, including a full register of every player to represent Great Britain - an honour that deserves to be recognised and honoured, a review of what's happened in the game in various parts of the world in 2004, and a huge selection of old pictures and memorabilia - including that old favourite among Rugby League fans, programme covers, which are sure to spark a few memories. We make no claims for this to be a comprehensive annual in the traditional manner - instead we see it merely as a collection of Rugby League nostalgia which we hope will bring a lot of pleasure to a lot of people as 2004 turns into 2005 - people like us who celebrate Rugby League history and folklore and don't want to forget the game they used to know.

Harry Edgar (Editor)

2004 The Season in Review

The 2004 season in England showed, just as it continues to do in Australia, that Rugby League is in very good shape when it concentrates on its strengths. In the Super League, when big guns collided, and especially when traditional local rivalries were involved, we saw thrilling Rugby League "played on the edge" and in front of big crowds. It may be a long way from all that Super League "world vision" we used to hear about, but whenever Leeds played Bradford or Wigan played St.Helens it was wonderful stuff - packed stadiums, hard-edged Rugby League played with a pace and ferocity that raises the passions of spectators and makes this a game like no other. Throw a Terry Newton or a Leon Pryce into the mix and those passions could be sent into overdrive.

Leeds led the way finishing the regular season a clear nine points ahead of second-placed Bradford, and in doing so pushed the average attendance at Headingley up by a huge 25% to a figure of 16,027. That was a tribute to both the enterprise of the Leeds club in promoting themselves in their city, and to the successful and entertaining football produced by their team. The recruitment of Australian Tony Smith as coach proved to be a masterstroke by Leeds, because his trademark soon became apparent on a team which began to play with an added aggression up front and a new and expansive dimension with the ball.

It wasn't just Leeds among the leading clubs who began to introduce much more ball movement and width to their attacking games, which made for a much more entertaining brand of football than that previously seen in this era of the 10-metre rule and its obsession with dummy-half and one-out running. The game in Super League definitely made advances on the field in 2004 - almost certainly helped by less pedantic behaviour by some referees - enabling the game to rediscover some of its physical edge and allow the good players to show just how skillful they were. And that was what the public wanted to see.

WAKEFIELD Trinity, along with Hull, were the biggest improvers of the Super League season as they managed to join the usual "big four" in the play-offs, and both were among the clubs who played entertaining and expansive football. Of course, both had the right players for creating a keep-the-ball-alive style of play in David Solomona at Wakefield and Jason Smith at Hull. They also both had excellent scrum-halves guiding them around the field in Ben Jeffries and Richard Horne. How Hull missed the injured Smith and Horne at the end of their season when they crashed out

of the play-offs at home to Wakefield. That was Trinity's big moment, in the top-six for the first time in their Super League life. And they almost went one better the following week when they went to Wigan and went down unluckily by just four points.

The play-offs as a whole really did take the game up a level - the sudden-death nature of knockout football plus the fact that they were played when there was a distinct Autumn chill in the air, added to the electricity of the atmosphere and an extra "bite" to the football.

Super League clubs continued to work extremely hard in marketing themselves, and overall were happy to report a further rise of around 8% in regular season attendances, taking the figure up to 8,570. Not only was that a new high since the advent of the full-time professional world of Super League in 1996, it was also the highest regular season average recorded since the introduction of two divisions to Rugby League in 1973. Closer inspection of those crowd figures reveal the increased average attendances were thanks largely to three clubs: Leeds, Wigan and Warrington - the latter enjoyed the feelgood factor of their new stadium (as Hull had done the previous year) and saw crowds go up a whopping 41% despite a less successful season of results compared to 2003. At the opposite end of the scale, away from the heartlands, London Broncos had the lowest crowds of all.

SEAN LONG - had both highs and lows in 2004.

BRADFORD'S Brian Noble finally got the nod to take over as Great Britain coach, and the Bulls enjoyed another "World Championship" after beating Aussie champs Penrith in the pre-season. The Bulls were also the club who provided a welcome back to Iestyn Harris when he decided he did not wish to stay in Welsh Rugby Union any longer. It provoked a messy slanging match with Leeds in the press. But it was St.Helens who found themselves creating most of the wrong kind of headlines after they went to Odsal on Easter Monday without 11 regular first-teamers. Worse was to follow when the *"Daily Mail"* took it upon themselves to reveal that two Saints players, Sean Long and Martin Gleeson, had put bets on St.Helens losing that game. It all ended in tears with both Long and Gleeson copping long suspensions - Gleeson eventually leaving Saints and being signed by Warrington in a rare big money transfer deal.

That turned 2004 into a bitter-sweet year particularly for Sean Long who in May became one of the few players to be awarded the Lance Todd Trophy for a second time as he inspired St.Helens to their win over Wigan in the Challenge Cup Final played in Cardiff.

CASTLEFORD were the club to draw the short straw in a battle to avoid last place in the Super League which involved London Broncos, Salford and eventually a straight shootout with Widnes. Cas', like Widnes, had sacked their coach mid-season and provided one of the most unexpected episodes in 2004 when they brought in Ellery Hanley to offer advice to their stand-in coach Gary Mercer. Ellery, the former Great Britain skipper, and a true legend of the game, didn't stick around too long and Cas' couldn't pull out of their losing habit.

Their relegation provoked all the usual comments from those with a vested interest (not from the good folk at the Castleford club themselves we hasten to add) that the game should scrap relegation for Super League clubs and clubs like Cas' were, quote: "too good to go down." Of course, nobody could argue with the claims that Castleford were a far stronger club commercially and in their off-field organisation than any that might replace them in 2005 by being promoted from National League One. But, had any of the National League clubs also had the luxury of receiving £850,000 per year and such high profile media coverage for the last nine years, it's a fair bet that they too could have done just as much work and become just as strong.

Perhaps those people in the media, especially on Sky television, who were crying crocodile tears at the prospect of Castleford being relegated as if there had been a death in the family, should consider just who has created this perception that going out of Super League is like dropping into a dark abyss - because in their eyes, you suddenly don't exist anymore.

Surely the way to avoid all this canned emotion, to ensure that relegation is not regarded as such a disaster, is to start evening up the current huge gap between the Super League and the lower division. Make the difference in central funding - currently a paltry £12,500 to National League One clubs compared to Super League's £850,000 - less extreme. Get Sky television to give the oxygen of publicity to the National Leagues by giving it some match coverage

The 2004 crop of Antipodeans with Wakefield were the most successful and popular imports to play for Trinity since a certain young Aussie called Wally Lewis came to Belle Vue 20 years ago. This picture is a reminder of Wally in action for Wakefield back then.

other than just its Grand Final, and at the very least to give their results out alongside the Super League results on their sports news bulletins.

Castleford fans needn't worry. They'll be okay because they are a real Rugby League club from a real Rugby League area. National League One is a very competitive and enjoyable league, and the presence of Cas' will make it even better. Just don't expect to see your results on the *"Rugby League channel"* on telly.

WIGAN, St.Helens, Leeds, Bradford, Hull and now the emerging Warrington and Wakefield Trinity continued to show the real strength of Rugby League in its heartland areas, and the same could be said at lower levels of the game where, for clubs out of the media spotlight of Super League, latent interest does not get translated into attendance levels. But for some clubs in traditional RugbyLeague areas people have just been waiting for a successful team to support and at York, Whitehaven, Workington and Barrow the growing return of interest and enthusiasm was a major positive in 2004.

Steady success at both York and Whitehaven, both clubs who almost disappeared in recent years only to be ressurrected by supporters who showed them a new way of running their affairs as community-based clubs, saw crowd levels continue to rise and also with big away followings which boosted the crowds when they went on the road. And Workington Town, a club that was down on its knees after being relegated to League Two and apparently on a downward spiral that nobody could stop, saw its base support shoot from a scary 500 back up to the 1,000 mark within a few weeks of new coach Ged Stokes creating a glint of hope for the team on the field. The other former north west giants, Barrow, felt a similar surge of enthusiasm as it became apparent they could win the League Two championship and thus claim a trophy for the first time in 20 years - to the point where Barow took around 1,000 fans with them to Dewsbury for the last game of their season. It may be small potatoes in Super League terms, but it was good to see.

OVERSEAS players played a huge role in most English Rugby League clubs, both in the Super League and in the National Leagues, with none making more impact that Bradford's huge Tongan/New Zealand winger Lesley Vainikolo. The man they call "the volcano" was the game's leading try-scorer in 2004 and surely one if its biggest drawcards.

Vainikolo might be the new Billy Boston and comparing present-day stars with those of the past is always fascinating, but often misleading because the game itself has changed so much. The old adage that great players would be great in whatever era they played, is probably the best one to believe in - because nobody can deny that the present day professionals have to be fitter, stronger and faster than those

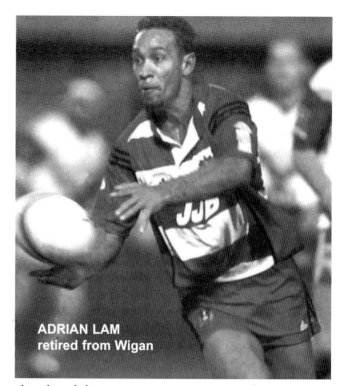

ADRIAN LAM
retired from Wigan

Lesley the Volcano

who played the game many years ago, and so many young players now are brought up being able to send spin passes 20 or 30 yards accross the field that you just never saw before Wally Lewis produced his masterpiece at Central Park in the 1982 Ashes Test match. Whether all that makes the game "better" is a moot point - it's just different - but what it does mean is that the gap between full-time professionals and semi-pros' has become insurmountable making Rugby League very much a two-tier sport both at club level in England and at international level.

2004 saw several of the game's greatest players say farewell and hang up their boots - none greater than in Australia where Brad Fittler retired at the top. Mighty Queensland forward Gorden Tallis also called it a day at the end of the season, whilst in England Adrian Lam called a halt on his playing days with Wigan. Scrum-half Lam had made an enormous contribution to Rugby League in his native Papua New Guinea, captaining the Kumuls in both 1995 and 2000 World Cups as well as captaining Queensland in State of Origin.

Whilst a whole raft of Antipodeans with Super League clubs were retiring, among them Hull's former New Zealand Test captain Richie Barnett, the Australian Jim Dymock who made such a big contribution to the London Broncos, and Tongan winger Tevita Vaikano who left Bradford to see out his playing days in Rugby Union, one of British League's best ambassadors, Mike Forshaw, retired after a final season with Warrington, and Darren Turner, one of the Sheffield Eagles heroes in their famous Wembley win in 1998, was forced to call a halt at Huddersfield with a knee injury. All will be missed.

Rugby League Journal Awards 2004

Our *"Rugby League Journal Annual"* awards for 2004 are given from the viewpoint of people who support the game at all levels. No prizes for the winners just the honour of knowing their efforts have been fully appreciated by the people who have been involved in the game at many different levels for many years. They have our respect.

In the Super League, four players in particular stood out: **Andy Farrell (Wigan)** for his unstinting physical effort and ability to raise his team when they needed him most. Farrell is a player, unlike so many Super League forwards, who still plays a full 80 minutes every game and moving up to the front-row did nothing to stifle his skills. **Lesley Vainikolo (Bradford)** for the sheer explosive excitement he brought to the game, one of those players who brings a buzz to the crowd everytime the ball goes near him. **Danny McGuire (Leeds)** likewise a player who gets the pulses racing with his pace and elusiveness and the way he has perfected one of the great joys of Rugby League through many generations - support play. Just like a Hardisty, a Millward, a Murphy or an Edwards of years gone by, whenever a break was made by a teammate young Danny would be on their shoulder and seconds later touching down for a try. **David Solomona (Wakefield Trinity)** one of those players you know is always going to produce a spectacular pass and keep the ball alive, he was one of the reasons behind Trinity's charge into the play-offs.

Our choice of coach of the year in the Super League would be torn between **Shane McNally (Wakefield Trinity)** and **Tony Smith (Leeds).** McNally for obvious reasons of turning Trinity from perennial strugglers into a top-six team (and one of the most good to watch sides in the competition), Smith for quite clearly changing the way Leeds played and improving individuals in it significantly.

Outside the Super League in National League One our player of the year is **Aaron Lester (Whitehaven.)** In a season which, in years to come, will be remembered as a golden age for Whitehaven, their captain-courageous Lester led them from the front yet again. This year he took less personal accolades as having the support of a talented lieutenant like Sam Obst in his side meant he didn't have to perform his "superman" tricks quite so often - but Lester was always the man driving his team forward and right in

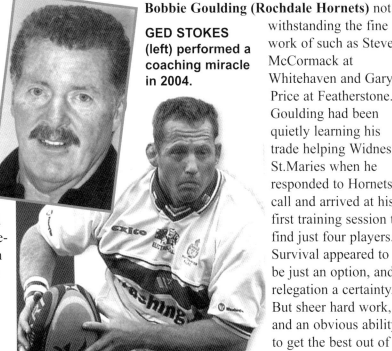

GED STOKES (left) performed a coaching miracle in 2004.

AARON LESTER (above) after eight years of leading from the front finally got to enjoy the feeling of success.

the thick of where the action was toughest - and had he not performed the same herculean efforts throughout the previous seven seasons there might not have been a Whitehaven club still going to enjoy such moments of success as they did in 2004.

Coach of the year in National League One goes to **Bobbie Goulding (Rochdale Hornets)** not withstanding the fine work of such as Steve McCormack at Whitehaven and Gary Price at Featherstone. Goulding had been quietly learning his trade helping Widnes St.Maries when he responded to Hornets' call and arrived at his first training session to find just four players. Survival appeared to be just an option, and relegation a certainty. But sheer hard work, and an obvious ability to get the best out of his lads, had Rochdale looking like a very useful side by mid-season.

In National League Two three key players we could not seperate: **James King (Barrow), Danny Brough (York)** and **Johnny Limmer (Workington Town.)** But no doubts over the coach of the year by a country mile, **Ged Stokes (Workington Town.)** What he achieved in 2004 is something those in the well financed world of Super League could hardly begin to comprehend. It was quite a coup for Workington to get the New Zealand assistant coach in the first place but, a bit like Bobbie Goulding at Rochdale, he found himself walking into a club on its knees. Town had few players, some they had were off playing Rugby Union, local amateurs wouldn't sign for them and the morale of what few supporters were left was at rock bottom, with crowds down to less than 500. In came Ged with an enthusiasm, realism and work ethic that began to change everybody's outlook. He had the personal contacts to be able to bring over three key players from New Zealand and the talent to mould a side who made a massive improvement. Town finished up going within one game of their Grand Final - and Stokes saved them.

HOW THEY FINISHED

FINAL LEAGUE TABLES
2004

SUPER LEAGUE

	P	W	D	L	F	A	Diff	Pts
Leeds	28	24	2	2	1037	443	594	50
Bradford	28	20	1	7	918	565	353	41
Hull	28	19	1	7	843	478	365	40
Wigan	28	17	4	7	736	558	178	38
St.Helens	28	17	1	10	821	662	159	35
Wakefield	28	15	0	13	788	662	126	30
Huddersfield	28	12	0	16	518	757	-239	24
Warrington	28	10	1	17	700	715	-15	21
Salford	28	8	0	20	507	828	-321	16
London	28	7	1	20	561	968	-407	15
Widnes	28	7	0	21	466	850	-384	14
Castleford	28	6	0	22	515	924	-409	12

NATIONAL LEAGUE ONE

	P	W	D	L	F	A	Diff	Pts
Leigh	18	14	0	4	686	407	279	28
Whitehaven	18	14	0	4	552	312	240	28
Hull K.R.	18	10	0	8	466	428	38	20
Oldham	18	10	0	8	482	503	-21	20
Featherstone	18	9	1	8	500	491	9	19
Doncaster	18	9	0	9	503	534	-31	18
Batley	18	8	0	10	478	469	9	16
Rochdale	18	7	1	10	472	587	-115	15
Halifax	18	7	0	11	426	492	-66	14
Keighley	18	1	0	17	366	708	-342	2

NATIONAL LEAGUE TWO

	P	W	D	L	F	A	Diff	Pts
Barrow	18	14	1	3	521	346	175	29
York	18	13	0	5	630	308	322	26
Sheffield	18	12	0	6	569	340	229	24
Swinton	18	12	0	6	547	460	87	24
Workington	18	10	0	8	597	479	118	20
Hunslet	18	10	0	8	475	394	81	20
Chorley	18	7	2	9	460	522	-62	16
London Skol.	18	6	0	12	361	583	-222	12
Dewsbury	18	3	1	14	284	595	-311	7
Gateshead	18	1	0	17	298	715	-417	2

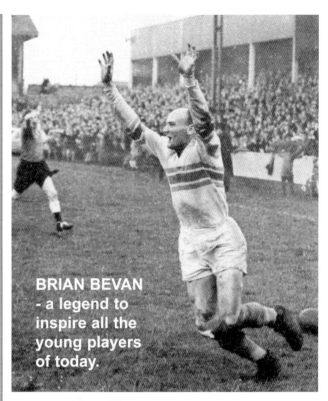

BRIAN BEVAN - a legend to inspire all the young players of today.

and the
DREAM TEAMS

(Official RFL merit teams for 2004)

SUPER LEAGUE

Shaun Briscoe (Hull): **Lesley Vainikolo** (Bradford), **Keith Senior** (Leeds), **Sid Domic** (Wakefield Trinity), **Marcus Bai** (Leeds); **Danny McGuire** (Leeds), **Richard Horne** (Hull); **Andrew Farrell** (Wigan), **Matt Diskin** (Leeds), **Paul King** (Hull), **Ali Lauitiiti** (Leeds), **David Solomona** (Wakefield T.), **Paul Sculthorpe** (St.Helens).

NATIONAL LEAGUE ONE

Jon Goddard (Oldham); **Rikki Sheriffe** (Halifax), **Mick Nanyn** (Whitehaven), **Matt Foster** (Keighley); **Mattie Wray** (Featherstone); **Tommy Martyn** (Leigh), **Sam Obst** (Whitehaven); **Makali Aizue** (Hull K.R.), **Paul Rowley** (Leigh), **Tommy Hodgkinson** (Rochdale), **Howard Hill** (Whitehaven), **Andy Spink** (Batley), **Craig Walsh** (Whitehaven).

NATIONAL LEAGUE TWO

Wayne English (Swinton); **Austin Buchanan** (York), **Chris Langley** (York), **Chris Maye** (Swinton), **George Rayner** (Hunslet); **Scott Rhodes** (York), **Darren Holt** (Barrow); **Rupert Jonker** (London Skolars), **Jonny Limmer** (Workington Town), **Ian Parry** (Chorley Lynx), **Andy Raleigh** (Sheffield), **James King** (Barrow), **Steven Bradley** (Gateshead).

WARRINGTON WELCOME

All Rugby League fans know they will be warmly welcomed to Warrington's new Halliwell Jones Stadium which saw the club's average home attendance rise by a remarkable 41% in its debut season of 2004. But trips to Warrington weren't always quite so comfortable in the days when Wilderspool was nicknamed "The House of Pain." Back in the late 1980s Warrington developed a fearsome reputation with a forward pack of real hard heads led by Kiwi enforcer Kevin Tamati and Australian tough guy Les Boyd (both pictured above wearing Warrington's primrose and blue.) "We were the bad boys team," remembers Tamati, now back home in New Zealand at the age of 50. "We also had Alan Rathbone, Les Davidson and Steve Roach. It was an awesome pack."

(Pictured left) another Warrington favourite in the 1980s, the prolific goal-kicker Steve Hesford.

ANDY FARRELL

FLASHBACK - to a young Andrew Farrell in action is his second Test match for Great Britain - a narrow win over France in 1994.

GREAT BRITISH RECORD

Unbroken decade of Tests for Wigan skipper

Farrell has carried the burden of expectancy as Great Britain's captain for eight years - as illustrated in the cutting (left) from the programme from his solitary Test match in Sydney against the Australians, a nightmare defeat, played on 12 June, 2002.

Andy Farrell now has his name proudly written in the history of British Rugby League as the man who has captained his country more times than any other individual. At the culmination of last year's Ashes series Farrell had skippered Great Britain no less than 24 times in Test matches, taking him well ahead of the previous holder of the record Ellery Hanley and such famous British leaders as Alan Prescott, Eric Ashton, Jonty Parkin, Roger Millward and Harold Wagstaff. Hanley captained Great Britain in 19 Tests, but Farrell - another man to become synonymous with the number thirteen jersey in the cherry and white of Wigan - overtook that record during the 2002 home series against New Zealand.

Andy first took over the captaincy of Great Britain in 1996 for the ill-fated Super League tour which took them to New Zealand, Fiji and Papua New Guinea - but not to Australia - and he has held it ever since in a remarkable unbroken sequence of 24 consecutive Tests as captain. In addition, Farrell also captained England in the year 2000 World Cup.

Even more remarkable, Andy Farrell has played in 29 consecutive Tests for Great Britain, not missing a single one since he made his full international debut against New Zealand in November 1993 - putting him insight of another British record, the 36 consecutive Tests and World Cup games played by Mick Sullivan between 1954 and 1961.

Farrell entered Test football as an 18-year-old in the second-row, and scored a try as Great Britain wrapped up a three-nil series win over the Kiwis with a 29-10 win at Headingley. In his second Test appearance, four months later in Carcassonne, he made the game safe for Great Britain in the closing minutes with a penalty-goal, controversially awarded by British referee Robert Connolly, as France were eventually beaten 12-4.

Farrell's Test debut was made in this Great Britain team at Headingley on 6 November, 1993: **Jonathan Davies** (Warrington); **John Devereux** (Widnes), **Gary Connolly** (Wigan), **Paul Newlove** (Bradford), **Martin Offiah** (Wigan); **Garry Schofield** (Leeds) captain, **Shaun Edwards** (Wigan); **Kelvin Skerrett** (Wigan), **Lee Jackson** (Sheffield Eagles), **Karl Fairbank** (Bradford), **Andy Farrell** (Wigan) **Chris Joynt** (St.Helens), **Phil Clarke** (Wigan). Substitutes: **Daryl Powell** (Sheffield Eagles), **Sonny Nickle** (St.Helens), **Alan Tait** (Leeds) and **Michael Jackson** (Halifax.)

Born on 30 May 1975, Andy Farrell joined Wigan from local BARLA club Orrell St.James as a 16-year-old after being capped as an English Schools international. Like so many of the greats in the history of British Rugby League he became a Test player whilst still a teenager. Andy played just five Tests before first captaining Great Britain, in 32-30 win over Papua New Guinea in Lae during the 1996 tour.

Like so many other fine British leaders in recent decades, he has never enjoyed the sweet taste of victory in an Ashes series with Australia, but particularly sad for Andy Farrell - who has led his country bravely from the front on so many occasions - playing in the era of summer rugby has denied him the opportunity of leading a full Lions tour to contest the Ashes in Australia. He has led Britain twice to Australia on ill-fated hit-and-run visits, for Tests in Brisbane in 1999 and Sydney in 2002, but how sad that a British captain with such a long record of service should be denied that ultimate honour in the annals of Rugby League.

13

McGuire keeps the tradition

Following in the footsteps of Mick Shoebottom and John Holmes

Danny McGuire - star of the 2004 season, hero of the Headingley thousands, one of the most stylish artists in the present day version of Rugby League. Yet a young man following a very familiar path in the footsteps of some of the favourite sons in the long and glorious story of the Leeds club.

Because, whilst Leeds have always been known as a glamorous club eager to recruit stars from around the world to parade before their Headingley public, their greatest eras of success in modern times have always been driven forward by local lads in the crucial half-back roles.

Step forward Danny McGuire in 2004. It was no coincidence that in the year Leeds finally came good to finish top of the Super League table by a clear nine points, was the year Maguire finally cemented a regular starting place at stand-off, bringing his team a fluent cutting edge with support play of the highest quality.

The emergence of young Danny's brilliance onto the biggest stage was something those Leeds fans who've watched their Academy over previous years had been eagerly waiting for - they had seen the future and his name was Danny McGuire.

And just like those wizards in the blue and amber number six jerseys before him, Mick Shoebottom and John Holmes, McGuire is a local city boy - a product of the East Leeds amateur club, where he learned his rugby and progressed through all the junior age-groups (encountering Leeds team-mate Rob Burrow on many occasions as an opponent from the Featherstone area in BARLA competitions) before being recruited by the Headingley scouts.

Mick Shoebottom (right) pictured with his half-back partner Barry Seabourne.

JOHN HOLMES - a true Leeds great.

Both the highly successful eras of the 1960s and 1970s for Leeds were achieved with local heroes Shoebottom and Holmes respectively at stand-off.

Whilst John Holmes was as local as any Headingley hero could ever hope to be - raised in the Kirkstall area - Mick Shoebottom was, strictly speaking, a Hunslet lad from south of the river in the city of Leeds. Both were teenage prodigies like Danny McGuire, Shoebottom making his first team debut at 17 and Holmes a mere 16. And both first learned their Rugby League at school before finding their way to the Loiners via a local amateur club.

Mick Shoebottom went to school at Low Road and played for the Hunslet Boys Club before joining Bison Sports amateur club. He played in seven major finals for Leeds between 1964 and 1970, including the victorious Wembley Cup Final in 1968 and the Championship Final the following year. John Holmes, meanwhile, was schooled at Burley Church of England and then Kirkstall County Secondary Schools and played for Kirkstall Boys Club. He played in no less than 19 major finals for Leeds between 1970 and 1984, including his inspirational performances in the winning 1977- and '78 Wembley finals.

No local boys could have done better for their home city than Mick Shoebottom and John Holmes - ironic that they should be found on the Headingley doorstep to fill the vital number six shirt whilst the club scoured the world for talent. Those with long memories at Leeds will be hoping Danny McGuire can achieve similar levels of success and longevity.

CUMBRIANS CRAVE COUNTY RETURN

It was after after some of the County's bigger names had retired and in a not very vibrant era for the game in Britain, but this Cumberland team from 1971 still managed to summon up the same underdog spirit and beat the stars of Lancashire 17-7 at Workington's Derwent Park. They are - with the clubs they were playing for at that time - left to right (Back row): Les Moore (Workington Town), Rodney Smith (Swinton), Eddie Bowman (Workington Town), Raymond Martin (Whitehaven), Graham McKay (Swinton) George Kirkpatrick (Hull K.R.), Bobby Blackwood (St.Helens), Tommy Thompson (Workington Town). (Front row): Louis Shepherd (Workington Town), Paul Charlton (Salford), Bob Nicholson (Workington Town), Jackie Newell (Workington Town), Rodney Morris (Whitehaven) and Howard Allen (Workington). The substitute forward missing from the picture was Raymond Morton (Workington Town). Cumbrian fans will know that Moore, Bowman and Shepherd were probably better associated with the Whitehaven club where they began their professional careers, but in 1971 they were with Workington.

Nobody else in Rugby League appears to want it, but most Cumbrians still crave the return of the County Championship. The chance for players who have made the grade with leading clubs in other parts of the country to come home and play together alongside the local lads in front of their own people, was always a motivating factor for the game in Cumberland since its earliest days. The spirit engendered was the same as which gave rise to Queensland's passion for a State of Origin contest in the Australian game - the scale may not be quite the same, but the principle most definitely was.

One of the most heart-warming occasions of 2003 was the revival of the Cumbria County team (after a gap of nine long years) to open the tour of the New Zealand Residents team. Over 4,000 people turned out at Whitehaven's Recreation

RUGBY LEAGUE COUNTY CHAMPIONSHIP
Recreation Ground, Whitehaven

Cumberland v Yorkshire
WEDNESDAY, 13th SEPTEMBER, 1972. Kick-off 6-15 p.m.

Determination! Rodney Morris, the powerful Whitehaven winger shows this Lancashire pursuer — and the referee — a clean pair of heels during Cumberland's fine victory at Workington last season.

Programme 5p

Ground to see a real blood and thunder thriller in which the Kiwis clawed back a 24-nil deficit in the last ten minutes against the tiring Cumbrians (several weeks out of season) to achieve a draw with the last kick of the match. And the Cumbrian County team was to live on in 2004 with a match against an Anzac X111 at Workington.

The County Championship was finally abandoned by the Rugby League after the 1982-83 season amid steadily declining interest and enthusiasm from the "big boys" of Lancashire and Yorkshire. For the record, Cumberland won the Championship on 16 occasions, the last two as Cumbria in 1980-81 and 1981-82. Lancashire won it 34 times and Yorkshire 24 times, with one win for Cheshire way back in 1901-02. Enthusiasm would run high in Cumbria for its return.

The First World Cup Winners

All that are left are fading old newspaper cuttings like the one above showing heroes Dave Valentine and Gerry Helme being carried shoulder high by jubilant team-mates at the Parc des Princes in Paris, and the memories of the survivors of that day 50 years down the line - like Phil Jackson, John Thorley, Jimmy Ledgard or Mick Sullivan. But it is a story that we will never grow tired of telling.

It was a beautifully sunny Autumn afternoon in Paris on 13 November 1954. The Parc des Princes was packed to near capacity with over 33,000 Frenchmen and women ready to enjoy an exhibition of the "new rugby" in their capital city which could bring sporting glory to their nation. France were already unofficial world champions after their victories on tour in Australia in 1951 and follow up wins over England, New Zealand and the Aussies again on French soil. Rugby League players like Puig-Aubert, Jackie Merquey and Jo Crespo were French sporting stars, and the World Cup tournament had been the dream made possible by the young and dynamic French Rugby League president Paul Barriere.

The British team had gone to the tournament - travelling by bus and ferry accross the channel - described as "no hopers" following the unavailability of a host of their international stars. Only three remained from the recently completed 1954 Lions tour - Dave Valentine, Gerry Helme and Phil Jackson. The 18-man squad had been allowed just two training sessions together at home before departing for the tournament in France under the guidance of coach Joe Egan, but he was not allowed to travel with them to the World Cup. But all the doubters reckoned without the inspirational leadership of the Scotsman Valentine who led his men with a call to arms by singing a Scottish folk song about a clan leader called "McPherson."

Great Britain's team of veterans, untried internationals and young rookies (some of whom, like Mick Sullivan, would go on to become major Test stars of the future) played superbly to beat Australia in Lyons, New Zealand in Bordeaux and draw with France in a 13-all thriller in front of over 37,000 fans who gathered for the first time in the new Toulouse stadium.

The World Cup Final came down to a re-match between France and Great Britain in Paris. Back home in England, fans who had access to that new thing called television gathered round to watch Valentine and his men go into action via the fledgling Eurovision link. It was the first time the British public had been able to watch live on television one of their own sporting teams playing in a World Cup overseas.

Inspired by Valentine and the wily Gerry Helme at scrum-half, the British boys won a magnificent victory by 16 points to 12, and the first World Cup was their's. The huge trophy carried around the Parc des Princes by Dave Valentine and his boys who wrote their names into history that November day in Paris 50 years ago. The thirteen heroes consisted of two Scotsman, a Welshman and ten lads from the north of England. They were: **Jimmy Ledgard** (Leigh); **David Rose** (Leeds), **Phil Jackson** (Barrow), **Alistair Naughton** (Warrington), **Mick Sullivan** (Huddersfield); **Gordon Brown** (Leeds), **Gerry Helme** (Warrington); **John Thorley** (Halifax), **Sam Smith** (Hunslet), **Bob Coverdale** (Hull), **Basil Watts** (York), **Don Robinson** (Wakefield) and **Dave Valentine** (Huddersfield).

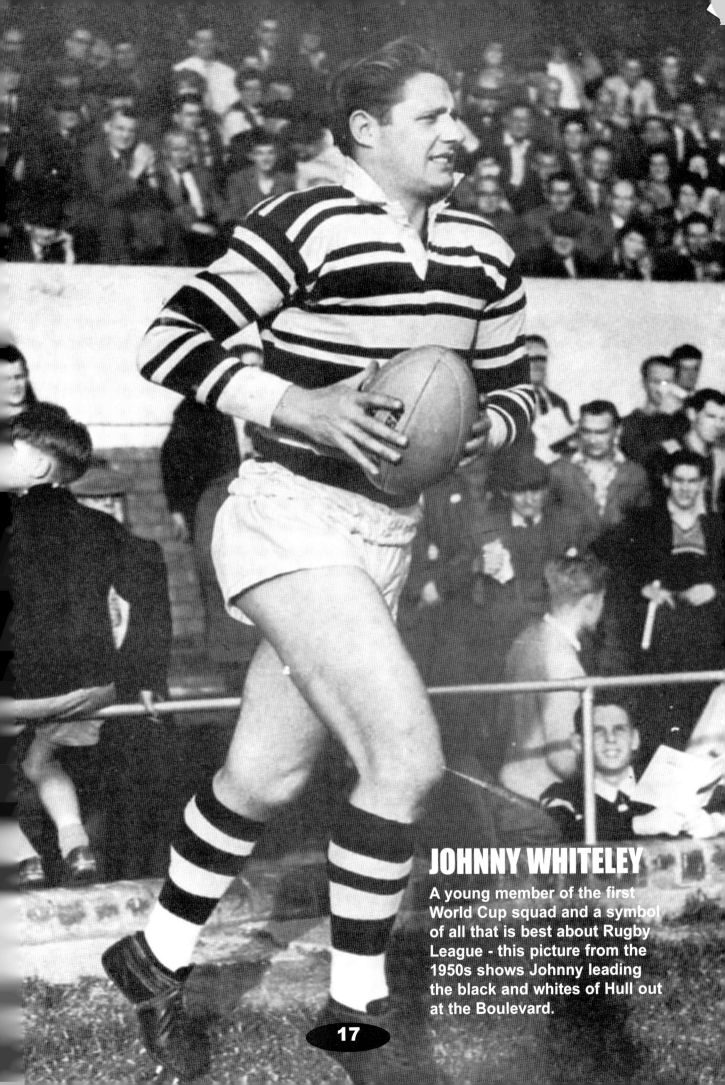

JOHNNY WHITELEY

A young member of the first World Cup squad and a symbol of all that is best about Rugby League - this picture from the 1950s shows Johnny leading the black and whites of Hull out at the Boulevard.

17

Glory Day

The RUGBY LEAGUE NEWS

FRANK MYLER
Great Britain's Captain

PHIL HAWTHORNE
Australia's Captain

AUSTRALIAN RUGBY FOOTBALL LEAGUE

THIRD TEST

AUSTRALIA
v.
GREAT BRITAIN

SYDNEY CRICKET GROUND

JULY 4, 1970

Registered in Australia for transmission by post as a newspaper

Vol. 51, No. 27

10c

It was American independence day in 1970 as Great Britain and Australia locked horns at the Sydney Cricket Ground in the third and deciding Test of that year's Rugby League Ashes series. The scene was one that had been enjoyed many times before - the atmosphere crackled with tension on the packed "hill" as the Australian team ran out in their green and gold colours. Equally familiar, the Great Britain team in their white with red and blue vees, walked slowly down through the Members Stand and onto the turf, just as they had strolled earlier from the Olympic Hotel accross the road and into the most famous arena in Rugby League's history. It was to be a day none of them would ever forget.

Bringing the Ashes back onto British soil as the 1970 Lions step onto the tarmac at Manchester airport. Coach Johnny Whiteley, captain Frank Myler and manager Jack Harding hold the Ashes cup aloft, with players Jimmy Thompson, Doug Laughton, Malcolm Reilly and Syd Hynes also in the picture.

Great Britain had lost only one game on their whole tour in Australia, a 37-15 hammering by the Aussies in the first Test in Brisbane, in a game marred by a wild brawl in which British prop Cliff Watson infamously re-arranged the face of his opposite number Jim Morgan. The general feeling afterwards was that the Poms had lost the game, but won the fight and the Aussie forwards were never quite the same again. Drastic measures were needed to save the Ashes after

that first Test defeat, just as they had been on the dramatic 1958 tour. Great Britain changed their team and turned things around with convincing 28-7 win in the second Test in Sydney - a match in which Roger Millward scored a record 20 points and the Aussies first came to appreciate the skills and power of the young loose-forward Malcolm Reilly. Two weeks later, on July 4th, came the decider. In another epic Test match Great Britain dominated the Australians, and whilst the final score of 21-17 meant the afternoon was tension-packed right to the final whistle, the truth of the matter was that the British scored five tries to one - and the Aussies' solitary touchdown, scored by Bob McCarthy, came from one of the most clear-cut cases of offside you could ever see on a Rugby League field.

Despite their superiority, which was every bit as strong as it had been in the 28-7 win in the second Test, Great Britain kept being pegged back by referee Don Lancashire awarding penalities which Australia's debutant full-back Alan McKean converted with great accuracy. The young Eastern Suburbs player kicked seven penalties to keep Australia in the game on the scoreboard. Fortunately he failed with just one kick, the conversion attempt to McCarthy's try from far out on the touchline, taken from almost exactly the same place on the Sydney Cricket Ground as that from which Ken Irvine landed a memorable conversion to deny Great Britain victory (and a clean sweep) in the third Test in 1962. Had McKean kicked that goal, Australia would have taken the lead 19-18 but he missed and moments later Roger Millward scored the try that sealed the game, running onto a pass from Douggie Laughton.

The Ashes were won and captain Frank Myler was carried shoulder high around the Cricket Ground. Nobody could ever have guessed that it would be the last time a British skipper would raise the Ashes cup in the 20th Century. In 2004, fully 34 years later, Frank Myler remains the last man to captain a winning British Ashes team, and it is a record Frank would dearly like to lose. And now nobody is quite sure when an Ashes series will be played again, so there are no immediate signs on the horizon that the drought can be broken. Undoubtedly, Great Britain had a heaven-sent opportunity in 2003 against an Australian team lacking so many first choice players, but still it didn't happen.

Frank Myler celebrated his 60th birthday in 2004 and was honoured by being made a Freeman of the Borough of Halton (his home town of Widnes) and again Frank expressed the hope that he wouldn't go down in history as the last British captain to win the Ashes. Of course, in the ensuing 34 years since that famous day in 1970, Rugby League has changed hugely and analysis of why the Aussies have maintained such a stranglehold could fill several books on many different areas of debate. There was a popular misconception that limited tackle football favoured the Australians

Great Britain winger Alan Smith attempts to tackle Australia's Ron Coote in a 1970 Ashes Test at the Sydney Cricket Ground.

compared to the old days when British teams with heavyweight packs had dominated the Ashes for 30 years - but the 1970 series was actually played under the controversial four-tackle rule.

Perhaps a clue about why Australian Rugby League made such progress in the modern era compared to the game in England could be gleaned from an article in the *"Rugby League News"* official programme for the third Test on July 4th, 1970. It was a report which commented on the dramatic growth of Rugby League in High Schools in Australia, describing it as "one of the most significant featues in the recent progress in our domestic football." An analysis of High School teams playing in organised competition Rugby League showed that there were nearly 43,000 players in New South Wales alone - 19,500 in the Sydney metropolitan area and a further 23,000 in the Country.

The contrast with what was happening in schools in England in 1970 - even in the game's heartlands in the north - could not have been more extreme. And perhaps here is a clue for those who still scratch their heads and wonder why it seemed all the new ideas in coaching trends, player preparation and promotion of the game in subsequent years came from the Australians.

The British team who won that third Test in 1970 and so brought the Ashes home was as follows: **Mick Shoebottom** (Leeds); **Alan Smith** (Leeds), **Syd Hynes** (Leeds), **Frank Myler** (St.Helens) Captain, **John Atkinson** (Leeds); **Roger Millward** (Hull K.R.), **Keith Hepworth** (Castleford); **Dennis Hartley** (Castleford), **Tony Fisher** (Bradford), **Cliff Watson** (St.Helens), **Doug Laughton** (Wigan), **Jimmy Thompson** (Featherstone Rovers) and **Malcolm Reilly** (Castleford.)

In the 21-17 victory, tries were scored by Atkinson (2), Hartley, Hynes and Millward, with Millward kicking three goals. The attendance was 61,258.

OH BROTHER

Pictured above are the smiling faces of the Beardmore twins, Bob and Kevin, enjoying Castleford's Challenge Cup victory at Wembley in 1986. Twins playing together at the very top level of Rugby League may remain a rarity - as well as the Beardmore boys there were the Rayne twins Keith and Kevin and the Drakes, Bill and Jim, who all played in Tests for Great Britain. And in the present day game there are the March brothers, David and Paul, of Wakefield Trinity and Huddersfield fame. In addition to the Raynes and the Drakes, other twins to play in Test football in the world of Rugby League were the Frenchmen Guy and Francis Laforgue and Aussies Kerrod and Kevin Walters. But the game's reputation as a family sport is illustrated on these pages by the full lists of all the sets of brothers to play internationals for the four major Rugby League Test playing nations: Great Britain, Australia, France and New Zealand.

GREAT BRITAIN

BATES, Alan and John
CHISNALL, David and Eric
CUNNINGHAM, Eddie and Keiron
DRAKE, Bill and Jim
EVANS. Jack and Bryn
FOX, Neil and Don
GORLEY, Les and Peter
HIGGINS, Alec and Fred
HILL, Cliff and David
HULME, David and Paul
MARTYN, Mick and Tommy
POLLARD, Charlie and Ernest
RAYNE, Keith and Kevin
REDFEARN, David and Alan
VALENTINE, Dave and Rob

AUSTRALIA

BURGE, Peter and Frank
BOLEWSKI, Mick and Henry
DIMOND, Bob and Peter
DOYLE, Joe and Ian
FARNSWORTH, Viv and Billy
GALLAGHER, Noel and Peter
GIBBS, Jim and Alf
JOHNS, Andrew and Matthew
LAIRD, Graham and Ray
McDONALD, John and Trevor
MESSENGER, Dally and Wally
MORTIMER, Steve and Chris
NORMAN, Ray and Rex
O'CONNOR, Alf and Frank
PLATZ, Lew and Greg
PROVAN, Norm and Peter
THORNETT, Dick and Ken
TYQUIN, Bill and Tom
VEIVERS, Greg and Mick
WALTERS, Kevin, Kerrod and Steve
WYNNE, Graeme and Peter

(Left) British Rugby League's most famous set of brothers - the Foxes of Sharlston, Don, Neil and Peter, pictured here in 1989 as Neil was inducted into the Rugby League "Hall of Fame." Don and Neil both won the Lance Todd trophy at Wembley and both played for Great Britain, touring together as Lions in 1962. Meanwhile elder brother Peter coached Great Britain in Test football and also coached Featherstone Rovers to victory in the Challenge Cup Final at Wembley.

(Right) One of the most prolific set of Rugby League playing brothers in the world - the Ropati family from New Zealand - pictured (left to right): Iva, Joe, Peter, Jerome, John, Feu and Tea. Of the seven brothers Iva, Joe and Tea played for the Kiwis, the same trio plus Peter all played professionally for English clubs and John was a New Zealand student international. In addition, the youngster Jerome - who was eight years of age when this picture was taken in 1987 - now plays for the New Zealand Warriors.

NEW ZEALAND

ASHER, Albert and Ernie
BAILEY, Garry and Roger
BELSHAM, Sel and Vic
BRIMBLE, Walter and Wilfred
BROWN, Len and Ray
CAYLESS, Jason and Nathan
CHASE, Rangi and Tom
DAVIDSON, Bill and Ben
HARRISON, Bill and Rata
HAYWARD, Henry and Morgan
HENRY, Whare and Whetu
HORO, Mark and Shane
IRO, Kevin and Tony
LOMAX, John and David
MITCHELL, Alf and George
MOUNTFORD, Bill and Ken
ORCHARD, Phil and Robert

PAUL, Henry and Robbie
ROBERTSON, Bruce and Morrie
ROPATI, Joe, Iva and Tea
SATHERLEY, Cliff and Jack
SCHULTZ, Bill and Paul
SORENSEN, Bill and Dave
SORENSEN, Kurt and Dane
SPENCER, George and John
TITTLETON, George and Wally
TUIMAVAVE, Paddy and Tony
WHITE, Jim and Pat
WRIGHT, Nick and Owen
WYNYARD, Dick and Bill

NOTE: Howie and Kevin Tamati and George and Duane Mann are cousins, not brothers.

FRANCE

BENAUSSE, Gilbert and Rene
BONAL, Elie and Jean-Marie
FRISON, Charles and Jean
GRANDJEAN, Christophe and Georges
GRUPPI, Jacques and Raymond
HATCHONDO, Jean and Louis
IMBERT, Jean-Marie, Jackie and Bernard
KAMINSKI, Etienne and Fernand
LAFORGUE, Guy and Francis
LASKAWIEC, Gabriel and Christian
MAJOREL, Roger and Joseph
SAVONNE, Andre and Gerard

WEMBLEY KNOCKOUTS

Wembley Cup Finals weren't just about glorious football and beautifully mown grass. They had no shortage of controversies as well - not least when teams had star players injured and forced off the field as these pictures show.

1 - Wigan full-back Colin Tyrer (who did not have the ball) hit by Castleford's Keith Hepworth in the 1970 Final. Tyrer left the field with blood pouring from a jaw injury.
2 - Workington Town stand-off Harry Archer cops a Mick Sullivan special in the 1958 Final. Archer was carried off concussed and Workington had to play a man short, going down 13-9.
3 - Alex Murphy carried off on a stretcher as Leigh won in 1971.

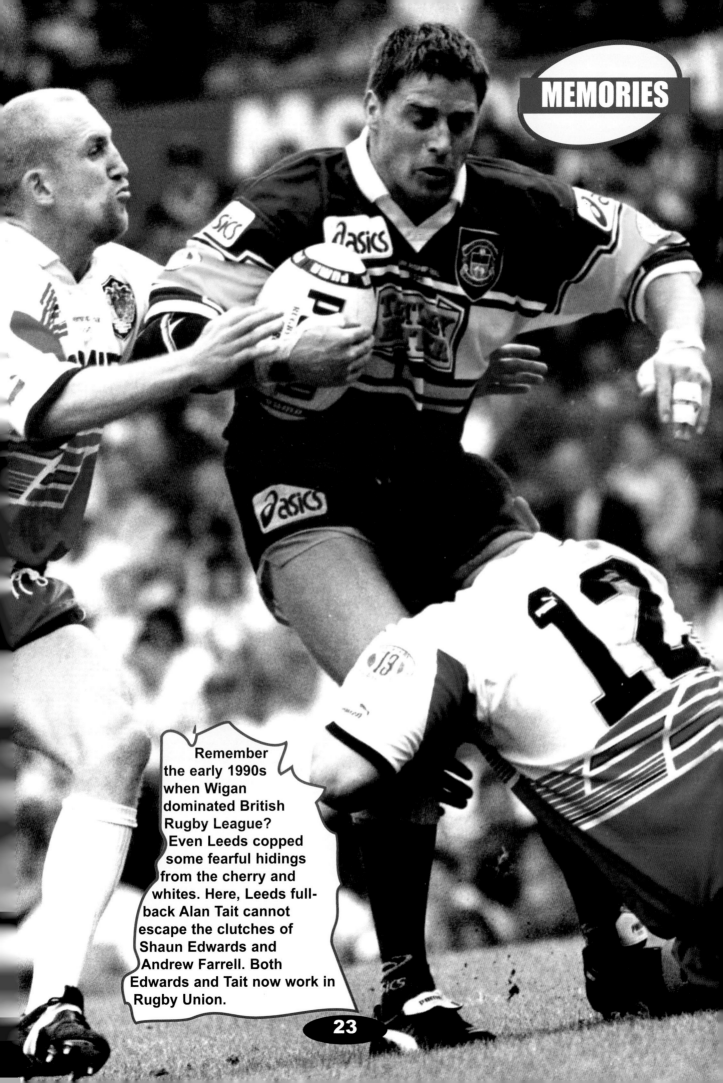

Remember the early 1990s when Wigan dominated British Rugby League? Even Leeds copped some fearful hidings from the cherry and whites. Here, Leeds full-back Alan Tait cannot escape the clutches of Shaun Edwards and Andrew Farrell. Both Edwards and Tait now work in Rugby Union.

ODSAL LEGENDS

JAMES LOWES

ROBBIE PAUL

Robbie joins the elite

It was back in July 1994 that Bradford Northern announced the signing of an 18-year-old lad from New Zealand named Robbie Paul. The signing of this "unknown" hardly made any headlines - Robbie was described as a full-back who had represented the Junior Kiwis, but his most news-worthy claim to fame appeared to be that he was the younger brother of Henry Paul who had already made an impression in England with Wakefield Trinity and was about to sign for Wigan in a swap deal for Andy Platt with the newly formed Auckland Warriors.

Who could have predicted that a decade later Robbie Paul would be firmly placed among the elite in the history of the Bradford club - up there alongside real Odsal Stadium legends of the past like Ernest Ward, Trevor Foster or Keith Mumby.

When Robbie arrived at Odsal it was hard to see where he might fit into the plans of then coach Peter Fox, but the teenager managed to get picked for ten first team games in his debut season, 1994-95. After that, everything changed at Bradford as Northern became the Bulls and the arrival of full-time professionalism gave clubs the kick up the backside they needed to get out and promote themselves. And nobody did it better than the Bradford Bulls.

The arrival of the Australian coaching team of Brian Smith and Matthew Elliott swept a new broom through the team on the field at Odsal, and Smith ensured that the off-field approach would be transformed by the appointment of Peter Deakin as the Bulls

Robbie the Kiwi.

head of marketing. Peter had learnt from American sports the value of building the profile of a club around what he called a *"franchise player"* - and nobody fitted that bill better for Bradford than Robbie Paul.

Immediately, Robbie became synonymous with the number one jersey at the Bulls and by September 1995 - at the age of only 19 - he was appointed the club captain, a role he has held ever since. Within the next 12 months Robbie had become the youngest captain ever to lead a team at Wembley in the Challenge Cup Final, and although Bradford were defeated by St.Helens Robbie won the Lance Todd trophy and became the first man in history to score a hat-trick of tries in a Wembley final.

With 11 seasons of service at Odsal behind him, including 10 of those as captain, in a glorious decade that has seen numerous Challenge Cups and Championships won by Bradford, the name of Robbie Paul can proudly be placed alongside the greatest legends in the club's history. Men like the Welshmen W.T.H. (Willie) Davies and Trevor Foster, forwards Frank Whitcombe and Ken Traill, New Zealanders Jack McLean and Joe Phillips, the little maestro of the 1960s revival years Tommy Smales, and wonderful servants like Ernest Ward and Keith Mumby.

Ernest Ward remains one of the true greats of

Rugby League. His career with Bradford Northern stretched from 1936 to 1953, during which he captained them to three successive Wembley finals and also led the 1950 Lions tour. In more recent times, Keith Mumby was the rock of Odsal, his 588 game career with Bradford was more than any other man in the club's history and he also captained the Great Britain Test team.

Bradford legends from earlier times - (left) the great Ernest Ward places the ball ready to kick one of the 538 goals he landed for Bradford Northern and (above) Keith Mumby, the man who played more games, kicked more goals and scored more points than any other player in the club's history.

Britain's Ashes quest

It's a staggering statistic to consider that no British Rugby League fans under the age of 50 have ever seen their country win the Ashes on home soil.

Great Britain's captain Jeff Stevenson receives the Ashes trophy in 1959 standing alongside a disappointed Australian captain, Keith Barnes.

In December 2004 it was fully 45 years since Great Britain defeated Australia 18-12 in the third and deciding Test of the 1959 series to retain the Ashes. As Britain's skipper Jeff Stevenson of York received the Ashes cup, nobody could ever have dreamt that almost half a century later the British public would still be waiting to see that feat repeated.

Great Britain did, of course, win the Ashes twice more after 1959 - both times in spectacular style on Australian soil in 1962 and 1970 - but looking back to their last triumph on home soil present day fans will find it hard to believe some of the headlines that dominated the newspapers after that deciding Test win in December 1959.

"We will never win a series here says Tour boss" was a headline fairly typical of the Ashes inquest in the press. That came after the Kangaroo touring team manager Colonel Jack Argent could not conceal his bitterness in his post-match comments after seeing the Aussies lose 18-12 at Wigan's Central Park.

He said: *"We will never win a series here as long as your players are allowed to play the ball as they do. Some of them actually faced the touchline as they played it - what chance had our boys of getting the ball under such circumstances?*

"It is putting mildly to say we are disappointed. We were told before leaving Australia that we could never win in England. Both Great Britain and France can win in Australia, but we can't manage it here."

Colonel Argent, who died in 2004 at over 90 years-of-age, was angry with what leading English journalist Eric Thompson described as *"Great Britain's farcical pretences at playing the ball fairly."* The Chairman of the Rugby League Council Mr. Bill Cunningham saw the Australians' point of view saying: "I think it is time we had a chat with the referees on this play-the-ball and made them realise we are not happy about it."

Meanwhile, well known reporter for the *"Daily Express"* Jack Bentley commented: "I am not blaming referee Eric Clay. The play-the-balls were no better, no worse, than those seen and suffered every Saturday. I reckon he did a good job in this flashpoint finale to the Test series. My only quibble is that on three occasions he pulled up the Kangaroos and gave them penalties when I believe he might reasonably have applied the advantage rule. The Aussies were very hot under the collar about that."

How ironic that the Australian team manager believed his country would never be able to win a series in England, when the subsequent 45 years have proved to be just the opposite. The Aussies have not

THE COBBERS ARE CLOBBERED

Sack cloth (no Ashes) for Aussies

12.12.59

ERIC THOMPSON'S
TEST REPORT

GREAT BRITAIN kept the Ashes in a rather disappointing anti-climax to the Test series before a low attendance of 26,000. The best football was saved for the closing stages. Previously it had been mainly a hard, forward tackling tussle but the "too slow" centre, Neil Fox, played well to claim 15 of the British points.

Reg Gasnier put his stamp on the game by carving out both Aussie tries — the last one being the highlight of a match in which "incidents" were frequent but were kept under control. Unfortunately, it kept any wing runs down to a minimum again.

Stevenson led Britain well.

The shock last minute Karalius

From about 50 yards, NEIL FOX atoned for his previous Test failures by landing a great goal

goa to reduce the arrears after Wilkinson had retaliated at some headwork near the British posts.

So far there hadn't been any spectacular back moves from either side. In the main it was

a warning and as the players wheeled away it was seen that Wilson had a stream of blood pouring down his face.

It was still far from a brilliantly spectacular affair and there was a trace

put Great Britain into a 13-2 lead in this ragged game and virtually ended Australian hopes of making history by snatching the Ashes—they had lost their chance in the second Test at Leeds, when it had been there for the asking.

determined

Ike Southward gets to grips with Australia's full back Barnes, stopping his progress in today's Test match at Central Park.

One example of how British fans read the news of our last Ashes triumph on home soil on 12 December 1959, this cutting of a newspaper report by Eric Thompson, one of the leading R.L. journalists of the time.

been able to lose in the "Mother Country." Remember they went fully 52 years (from 1911 to 1963) without ever winning the Ashes in England. Obviously, the rules of the game, their interpretations and the way the game is refereed, have changed substantially between 1959 and the present day and perhaps the warning signs were on the wall for British Rugby Leage even as they won the Ashes 46 years ago.

Journalist Eric Thompson wrote: *"Great Britain have retained the Ashes, so all should be well. But, for me, doubts linger and the victory is rather hollow. Of the three Tests we have won two, but the Aussies have been the better football team in two Tests and have produced the new exciting names. We have not produced a new player of Test quality, and having deserted our normal open style in panic after the first Test defeat, have been anything but standard-bearers of a better football movement."*

Not everyone might fully agree with that assessment because the 1959 series had seen at least two new faces emerge in the Great Britain team, the Wakefield Trinity duo of centre Neil Fox and full-back Gerry Round - but whilst British scrum-half and captain Jeff Stevenson won praise for the way he had opened up play in the second Test at Headingley (won 11-10) the critics were no so happy at the way he had "clearly signposted the way to victory by frequently turning the ball back to the forwards" in the decider at Wigan.

Other controversial headlines after the game which saw Britain clinch the Ashes, which also would bring looks of amazement from younger fans today, centred around the live television broadcast of the third Test.

"Be warned: ban TV"... "Clubs blame TV for gate slumps"... "Live TV is gate killer" were typical of the banners accross the newspaper sports pages. As we look at the way international Rugby League in 2004 is effectively controlled by Sky television schedules it is hard to comprehend the volume of hostility towards live broadcasts in those early days of TV coverage. The concerns came to a head after a "disappointing" crowd of just 26,000 attended the deciding Tests - the lowest crowd of the three Tests in that series. Veteran journalist Tom Longworth commented that "40,000 were expected for the Test, and at the same time only 30,036 fans watched the 14 Championship matches played on the same afternoon." The Rugby League received a fee of £1,250 from the BBC for being able to broadcast the third Test live.

For the record, the Great Britain team who won the Ashes that day on 12 December 1959, was: Gerry Round (Wakefield); Ike Southward (Oldham), Eric Ashton (Wigan), Neil Fox (Wakefield), Mick Sullivan (Wigan); David Bolton (Wigan) Jeff Stevenson (York) capt.; Abe Terry (St.Helens), Tommy Harris (Hull), Jack Wilkinson (Wakefield), Brian McTigue (Wigan), Don Robinson (Leeds) and Johnny Whiteley (Hull).

The legend of the

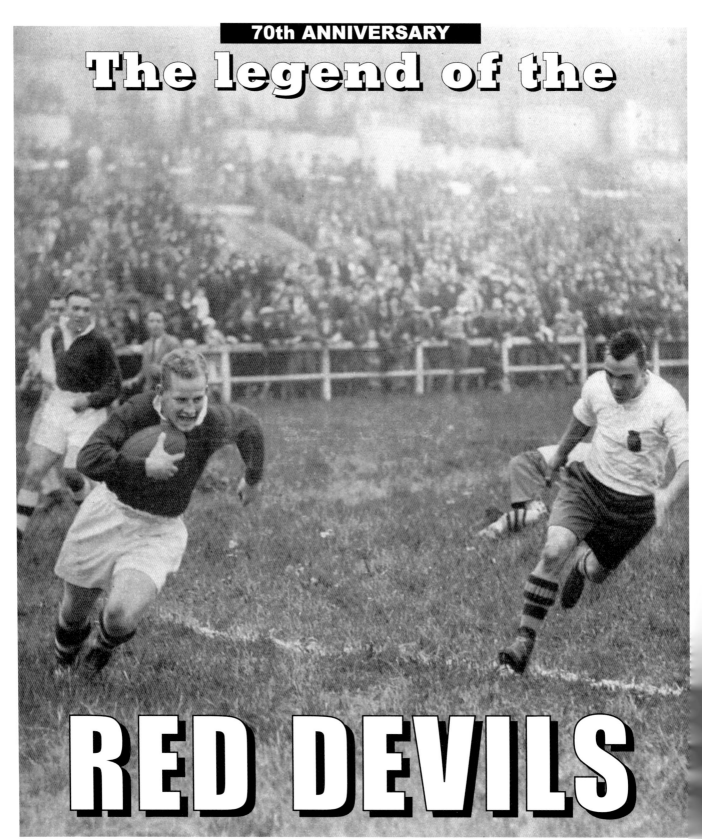

RED DEVILS

October 2004 marked the 70th anniversary of the birth of one of Rugby League's most enduring legends - the Red Devils. To be precise, it was Sunday, 21st October, 1934 when that famous name was first bestowed on the men of Salford as they became the first English club side to play Rugby League on French soil. The opening game of a six match tour which was to have such an inspirational effect on the launch of the *"new rugby"* in France was played in Paris and the programme welcomed the English visitors as *"Les Diables Rouges"* - the Red Devils.

Salford's famous team manager at the time, Lance Todd, was always quick to grasp an opportunity to promote the game and he ensured the name stuck with his club. Todd had taken Salford accross the channel at the invitation of the French who wanted the leading club in England to demonstrate the skills of the new game to an eager audience. A few months earlier Jean Galia has brought his team of French pioneers to England and one of their games had been against Salford at the Willows.

The original Red Devils tour itinerary and pioneering spirit of the Salford team would be quite mind-boggling for British Rugby League people in the 21st Century. They had set out for France on Saturday 20th October, 1934 immediately after winning the Lancashire Cup Final against Wigan at Swinton - there was no time for Gus Risman and his men to celebrate as they made a hectic dash from Station Road into Manchester city centre just in time to catch the 5.45 pm train from what is now Piccadilly station to London Euston. From London they joined the boat train to Folkestone to catch the ferry for the 1.15 am channel crossing to Dunkirk.

It was around 5.30 on the morning of Sunday 21st October when Messrs. Todd, Risman and their team stepped off the ferry and onto French soil. A further four hour train journey to Paris followed and they arrived at their hotel in the French capital in time to take lunch at mid-day, before proceeding to La Courneuve - an old racecourse on the outskirts of the city - where they were to play the Paris X111.

After some 16 hours of travelling and little sleep, no less than 11 of the 13 Salford players stepped out to play in France just 24 hours after competing in a fierce cup final against Wigan. They received a tumultuous welcome from the Parisien crowd - over 7,000 of them - who had flocked to La Courneuve to see the English exponents of the *"new rugby"* in defiance of the Rugby Union authorities who had done their best to place obstacles in the path of Rugby League by ensuring more accessible stadiums were made unavailable to the *"Treizistes."*

Despite their travel fatigue, the newly christened Red Devils thrilled the spectators in an exhibition style match which finished with a 51-36 scoreline in favour of Salford. Scrum-half Billy Watkins scored their first try on French soil and Gus Risman kicked their first goal - among the eleven tries scored against Paris was the one pictured on the page opposite by stand-off-half Emlyn Jenkins. In this very rare photograph from 70 years ago we can see the large crowd packed into the grandstand at the stadium in the Paris suburbs as Jenkins crosses the line and begins to run around behind the posts.

From Paris, the Red Devils' tour headed south by train to the city of Lyon where, on Saturday 27 October, Salford played the Lyon-Villeurbanne club. Like Paris X111 and the other four opponents they were to visit on the tour - Beziers, Albi, X111 Catalan and Villeneuve - Lyon-Villeurbanne were founder members of the new French Rugby League which was just beginning its inaugral season.

Salford won 34-17 in Lyon, and 24 hours later they beat Beziers 41-8 following another 200 mile train journey. At Beziers 6,000 spectators came to watch them play on a dustbowl pitch hastily converted from a

vineyard after the Rugby Unionists, again, had ensured the local stadium was out of bounds. The Australian pioneer Harry Sunderland, who accompanied the Salford tour, reckoned such unsporting behaviour did much to endear the *"new rugby"* to the French public.

Three further wins were achieved in the space of four days at Albi (44-6), at Perpignan against the X111 Catalan (41-16) and at Villeneuve (34-10), with an all-day bus journey from Perpignan to Villeneuve-sur-Lot sandwiched in between. Salford arrived back in Manchester late on the evening of Tuesday, 6 November 1934 proud to have played their part in rugby history. But it was a further 19 years before the Red Devils Association was formed, initially by four members of the team on that 1934 French tour - Emyln Jenkins, Gus Risman, Barney Hudson and their captain Billy Williams - and made open to all Salford players involved in the club during the management of Lance Todd. In later years membership was made open to all post-war Salford players, directors and staff.

FARTOWN'S CUP GLORY

HUDDERSFIELD WIN AT WEMBLEY

Pictured above, the joyous sight of the claret and gold of Huddersfield victorious at Wembley in 1953 after beating St.Helens in the Challenge Cup Final - it was the last time Fartown won the cup. Their captain Russ Pepperell is chaired by his happy team-mates alongside Peter Ramsden who had celebrated his 19th birthday by scoring two tries and winning the Lance Todd Trophy. Huddersfield beat St.Helens 15-10 to win the cup.

Challenge Cup in 2004 to St.Helens

St.Helens played in the very first Challenge Cup Final way, way back in 1897. The Saints were beaten by Batley that day and it was to be fully 59 years before they finally got their hands on Rugby League's most famous trophy by winning the 1956 Final at Wembley against Halifax. Alan Prescott captained Saints that momentous day in their history and no shortage of subsequent St.Helens skippers have followed in his footsteps by carrying off the Cup - among them men like Vince Karalius, Alex Murphy, Kel Coslett, Chris Joynt and Bobbie Goulding.

The Challenge Cup in 2004 found its way to Knowsley Road once again after the Saints 32-16 victory in the Final over fierce rivals

Saints are no strangers to lifting the Cup in the sun against the old enemy from Wigan - flashback to glorious Wembley in 1961 as skipper Vince Karalius is hoisted aloft by his fellow forwards Cliff Watson, Dick Huddart, Bob Dagnall and Abe Terry, with Alex Murphy just appearing on the left.

Wigan. Played on a blisteringly hot day in Cardiff - the second of a trio of Rugby League Challenge Cup Finals scheduled for the Millennium Stadium before the much anticipated return to Wembley - St.Helens scored their first try as early as the third minute and had dominant forces in scrum-half Sean Long and captain Paul Sculthope. Long's pace and kicking ability proved the difference and he was selected as the Lance Todd Trophy winner, thus becoming only the fourth player to win the coveted award twice. Saints had led Wigan 20-10 at half-time in front of a capacity crowd of 73,734.

Whilst the Final of the 2004 Challenge Cup had its usual colourful big-event atmosphere, the semi-finals had little of the tenseness associated with such games in years gone by - Wigan beating a generous Warrington team 30-18 and St.Helens thrashing Huddersfield 46-6 - hard to believe such a scoreline in a Challenge Cup semi-final. In the quarter-finals Wigan beat Wakefield Trinity 20-4, St.Helens beat Hull 31-26 in a thriller, whilst two teams from the lower divisions found the pace and power of Super League opposition ultimately too much for them - York losing 50-12 at Huddersfield and Whitehaven going down 42-10 to Warrington in a match which was televised live on BBC and proved to

be an uplifting occasion.

It was the fifth season in a row that the two Cup Finalists had come from Super League's "big four."

2004 POWERGEN CHALLENGE CUP FINAL

At the Millennium Stadium, Cardiff
Saturday, 15 May 2004
ST.HELENS 32 beat WIGAN 16
St.Helens: Tries: Gilmour, Talau, Wellens, Sculthorpe.
Goals: Long (6)
Wigan: Tries: Newton, Dallas (2). **Goals:** Farrell (2)

ST.HELENS TEAM:
Paul Wellens; Ade Gardner, Martin Gleeson, Willie Talau, Darren Albert; Jason Hooper, Sean Long; Nick Fozzard, Keiron Cunningham, Keith Mason, Chris Joynt, Lee Gilmour, Paul Sculthorpe (Capt.) *Substitutes:* Mark Edmondson, Dom Feaunati, Jon Wilkins and Ricky Bibey.
WIGAN TEAM:
Kris Radlinski; David Hodgson, Sean O'Loughlin, Kevin Brown, Brett Dallas; Danny Orr, Adrian Lam; Craig Smith, Terry Newton, Quentin Pongia, Danny Tickle, Gareth Hock, Andrew Farrell (Capt.) *Substitutes:* Terry O'Connor, Danny Sculthorpe, Mick Cassidy and Stephen Wild.
Referee: Mr. Karl Kirkpatrick (Warrington)
Attendance: 73,734 (capacity)
Lance Todd Trophy winner: Sean Long (St.Helens)

John Wolford leads a happy Bramley out at McLaren Field.

Kel Coslett in his early days after joining Saints from Wales. Kel was a full-back who eventually made his way into the pack and captaining St.Helens at Wembley in the Cup Final.

COMPETITION - THE EYES HAVE IT

WIN HISTORIC RUGBY LEAGUE VIDEOS

If you correctly identify the four famous former players pictured by their eyes (below) you can win one of ten prizes of three videos each from the "Open Rugby Nostalgia" catalogue of historic R.L. videos.

A

Clue: Coach

B

Clue: Kiwi

C

Clue: Winger

D

Clue: Aussie

All four, A,B,C, and D, played for English clubs in the 1980s.

The first ten correct entries drawn will receive their choice of three videos from the "Open Rugby Nostalgia" catalogue which includes over 100 historic Rugby League videos. Send a first class stamp to the address below to receive a free catalogue.

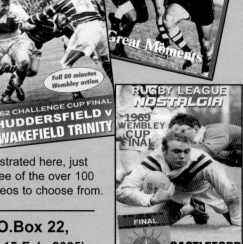

Illustrated here, just three of the over 100 videos to choose from.

Send your entries to: Quiz, Rugby League Journal, P.O.Box 22, Egremont, Cumbria, CA23 3WA. *(Closing date for entries 15 Feb. 2005) Winners will be announced in issue 10 of Rugby League Journal - out March '05.*

CLUB FILES

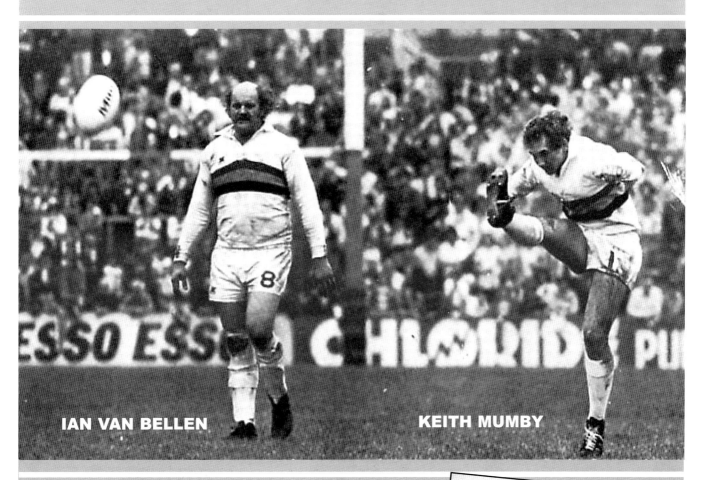

IAN VAN BELLEN   KEITH MUMBY

On the following pages you can enjoy files on all the pro' clubs including memorabilia, team photos and annual reports on the 2004 season.

Flashback to Barrow's last major trophy win in the 1983 Lancashire Cup Final - see Barrow forward Steve Herbert on the attack and making light of the presence of several Widnes defenders. The Chemics players in the picture are: Tony Myler - making the tackle - Joe Lydon, Eric Prescott, Fred Whitfield, Eric Hughes and Steve O'Neill. Barrow won a memorable victory to take the Lancashire Cup at Wigan's Central Park.

ANNUAL REPORT
2004

BRAVO Barrow - winners of the National League Two championship title in 2004. It was great to have some silverware at Craven Park again for the first time since the Barrovians' famous Lancashire Cup win of 1983. And the Furness public showed they would respond to success when around 1,000 fans travelled to Dewsbury for the final and title-deciding match of the season.

With the popular Peter Roe back as coach, Barrow's success was built on the talented Aussie duo in the pack, Dave Clark and James King, the physical presence of ex-BARLA international prop Stuart Dancer, the youthful promise of Paul Jones and Barry Pugh, the experience of 10-year veteran Phil Atkinson and the kicking skills of the returning Darren Holt.

Barrow will celebrate their most famous anniversary in 2005 as it will be 50 years since they won the Challenge Cup at Wembley. In the half century that has passed from 1955 to 2005 many things have changed for Barrow-in-Furness and their Rugby League club which brought such prestige to the town, especially in the decade of the fifties when they contested three Wembley Finals in the space of six years. But one thing that can never be taken away from Barrow is that wonderful history which is now celebrated with a statue of their talisman and inspiration, Willie Horne. The statue stands close to the Craven Park ground where Willie and his team thrilled thousands of Barrovians with their successes during the 'fifties.

Willie Horne leads Barrow with the Challenge Cup at Wembley after their win in the 1955 Final.

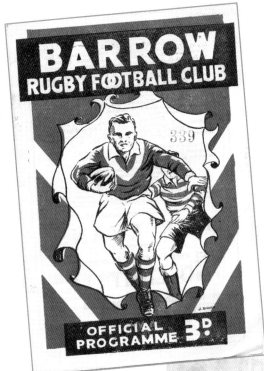

BARROW RUGBY FOOTBALL CLUB

339

OFFICIAL PROGRAMME 3D

Pictured (left) is a sight that will be remembered by those who were young Barrow fans in the late 'fifties and early 'sixties, something that greeted them every other Saturday as they walked along Duke Street or Hindpool Road on their way to Craven Park. The distinctive Barrow programme, with the picture of the player bursting out of the front cover clad in the blue jersey with the white vee which signified "Barrow" to everybody in the world of Rugby League. Craven Park remains a treasure in the game, an old fashioned "traditional" ground, covered on all four sides and within easy walking distance of the town centre. The new grandstand is named after Willie Horne and the touchlines close to the perimeter walls still trace the footsteps where great wingers like Jimmy Lewthwaite, Frank Castle and Bill Burgess once flew in at the corner for tries. The Barrow team in 2004 have carved their own bit of history by winning their Divisional Championship - in an area which has some of the longest established Amateur Rugby League clubs in the country, Barrow will always be a stronghold for the game.

(Right) Tommy Bishop playing for Barrow in a Challenge Cup tie at Wigan in 1965. By the end of the following season Tommy was a Wembley winner with St.Helens and in the Great Britain touring team to Australia. Also in the picture Wigan loose-forward Roy Evans and scrum-half Frankie Parr (right) whilst Barrow's Ivor Kelland rises from the front-row of the scrum.

On the way to Wembley - this was the Barrow team before their 1955 Cup semi-final win over Hunslet at Central Park, Wigan. Left to right (Standing): Frank Barton, Jimmy Lewthwaite, Les Belshaw, Reg Parker, Phil Jackson, Vince McKeating, Dennis Goodwin. (In front): Jack Grundy, Frank Castle, Willie Horne (Captain and coach), Ted Toohey, Clive Best and Bill Healey. Barrow win 9-6.

From Gallant Youths to Bulldogs, the story of Batley Rugby League Club is one that will always fascinate historians of the game. Founder members of the Northern Union, in 1897 they became the very first winners of the Challenge Cup - the famous trophy made by Fattorinis of Bradford which came to fire the excitement of the game's followers like no other in the ensuing years.

Batley beat St.Helens 10-3 in the first Challenge Cup Final which was played at Headingley in front of an attendance of 13,492 people who paid receipts of £624 17s 6d. A year later the Gallant Youths were back at Headingley to retain the Challenge Cup, beating Bradford 7-nil in the second Final of the competition, and this time the crowd had risen to over double the previous year, to 27,941- by far the biggest ever to attend a Northern Union match at the time. It is interesting to note that for both the following years' Challenge Cup Finals, in 1899 and 1900, when the venue was switched to Manchester and Batley were involved in neither, the crowds dropped back to less than 16,000 and 18,000 respectively - but in 1901 when Batley returned to Headingley to win their third Challenge Cup Final in five years, the attendance shot up again to set another new record at 29,563 - and there was no local Yorkshire derby involved as Batley's opponents were Warrington. Undoubtedly, the Gallant Youths were the glamour boys and the big crowd pullers of the game in those early days. And a second great era of success followed in the 1920s which included winning the Rugby League Championship in 1923-24.

From those early day heroes like Wattie Davies, Jack Goodall then Frank Gallagher, to Jack Perry, Norman Field, John Etty on to big Trevor Walker, Carl Gibson and modern days stars like Glen Tomlinson and now Barry Eaton, the youths of Batley have always been Gallant.

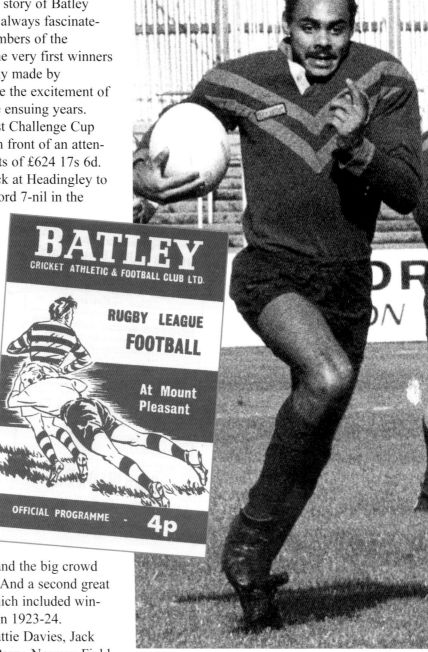

Carl Gibson pictured in action as one of Batley's most gallant youths - he played for Great Britain in 1985 as a Batley player before being signed by Leeds.

ANNUAL REPORT
2004

WITH Gary Thornton in his first season as head coach, Batley started 2004 like a house on fire. But a mid-season slump in form saw them drop from top-four candidates in National League One towards the relegation zone. Then the Bulldogs picked themselves up enough to finish in seventh place with a flourish. Their talented captain Barry Eaton was Batley's inspiration, guiding them from scrum-half as always and also working behind the scenes as the club's development officer. Other top performers were loose-forward Ryan Horsley, forwards Andy Spink, Tim Spears and Steve Hill, hooker Kris Lythe. pacy winger Bryn Powell and the very capable Mark Sibson at full-back. With Mount Pleasant one of the most improved stadiums in the National League, Batley should be a good side to watch in 2005 - if only they could attract the kind of crowds they deserve back to the Mount.

The year 2004 marked the 40th. anniversary of the birth and death of Bradford Northern. Yes, it's hard for the young fans of such a vibrant club as the Bradford Bulls are today to believe, but back in 1964 their team dropped out of the Rugby League in mid season, unable to continue as crowds in the vast Odsal bowl had dwindled to just 300 or so people. In the early post-war years Bradford Northern had been one of the most successful clubs in the game and it was unthinkable that they should just disappear. That's when the club's former full-back, New Zealander Joe Phillips, aided by the great Welsh forward Trevor Foster, stepped in and reformed the club in the summer of 1964. By the third week in August the new Northern were ready to play the first match at Odsal against Hull K.R. *(see the programme, right)* and the crowd had rocketed from 300 to over 13,000. Success came quickly with Tommy Smales at the helm and Trevor Foster remains a hugely respected man in the city of Bradford as the club they now call the Bulls celebrate the 40th anniversary of their re-birth.

(Above) Bob Haigh the great try-scoring forward in action for Bradford with Alan Redfearn in support.

Tommy's team - this was the Bradford Northern side which brought great joy to their followers so soon after their reformation in 1964 and won the Yorkshire Cup in 1965. Left to right (Standing): Terry Clawson, Lord, Ashcroft, Alan Hepworth, Lionel Wiliamson, Johnny Rae, Terry Ackerley, Jack Hirst. (Seated): Mike Brown, Dave Stockwell, Hardcastle, Tommy Smales (Captain), Gil Ashton, Morgan, Ian Brooke, Alan Rhodes. (In front): Davies and Willis Walker.

ANNUAL REPORT
2004

BRADFORD timed their run of form to perfection in 2004, playing in their fourth Grand Final in successive years after a regular season in which the Bulls aura of invincibility had taken a few jolts - even at Odsal. The Kiwi contingent was again at the heart of Bradford's play with Lesley Vainikolo a powerhouse on the wing and finishing as Super League's top try-scorer. Shontayne Hape came of age and Robbie Paul, in his 10th year with Bradford, showed no signs of slowing down. The signing of Iestyn Harris also promises much for 2005.

This was the Castleford team wich took them to Wembley and the Challenge Cup in 1970 for the second year in a row. Left to right (Back row): Ian Stenton, Brian Lockwood, Bill Kirkbride, Dennis Hartley, Malcolm Reilly,Mick Redfearn, Clive Dickinson, Tony Miller. (In front): Trevor Briggs, Tony Thomas, Alan Hardisty (capt.), Keith Hepworth, Derek Edwards, Alan Lowndes and Danny Hargrave.

(Above) memories of Wheldon Road.

Glory days for Cas' as Steve Norton and Malcolm Reilly carry the Challenge Cup around Wembley in 1970 after beating Wigan. On the left is Lance Todd Trophy winner Bill Kirkbride.

ANNUAL REPORT
2004

CASTLEFORD will not look back on 2004 with much pleasure. It was a year when they discovered the downside of the modern world Rugby League has created for itself - no sooner had they finished in the relegation spot than their team was being broken up as their best players were cherry-picked by other Super League clubs. For a club that has always made much of its family image and community spirit, it was a cruel way to discover what life can be like for clubs outside the chosen twelve. Cas' began the season with Graham Steadman as coach, when he left assistant Gary Mercer took on the reins and, for a brief period, was assisted by Ellery Hanley. None could turn things around for a Cas' team that laid much of the blame for their predicament at poor recruitment of older players for 2004. In the event, it was the oldest of all, Brad Davis, who returned from France and gave them some hope of an escape route. It wasn't to be, Cas' finished bottom and and will be in League One in 2005.

Classy Cas

The slogan "Classy Cas" first came into Rugby League in the 1960s when, with Alan Hardisty at the helm and wearing those all gold jerseys, Castleford began to emerge as one of the most attractive teams in the game. And the motto stuck well into the 'eighties when Cas' went back to Wembley to win the Challenge Cup under the captaincy of John Joyner. Castleford beat Hull K.R. in a Cup Final with a nail-biting finish in 1986 - the last time Cas' won at Wembley, and Joyner proudly lifted the trophy (pictured.) John was a classic Rugby League centre, who in later years played well at both stand-off and loose-forward. A local lad, he gave great service to Castleford over 19 seasons and to his country in an international career that stretched from 1978 through to 1984 in Test matches plus a call-up for the 1988 Lions touring team.

(Above) John Joyner on Great Britain duty. He played in 14 Tests for his country.

Flashback to Chorley Borough's first competitive match under that name, in August 1988 at Hunslet. There are some familiar faces on this Chorley team, including Steve Donlan, Carl Briscoe, Darren Abram, Bob Eccles, Mark Sheals, Steve Garner, Mike Smith, Tony Hodson and Dennis Ramsdale. Also there are long-serving former Blackpool Borough director George Lunn and Chorley club chairman Sid Secker.

The news that Chorley Lynx faced closure at the end of the 2004 season was set to create another chapter in the long and winding road of this little club that has played in a variety of different guises. And wouldn't it be ironic if the place to give the Lynx sanctuary turned out to be Blackpool? Because it was when the much loved old Blackpool Borough club left the seaside back in 1987 that the saga began that was to eventually lead to Victory Park, Chorley - calling at many stops along the way. Blackpool turned intially into Springfield Borough (playing in Wigan) but left after just one season for the new Chorley Borough to be formed in 1988. Not that the current Chorley Lynx is a direct descendant of that, strictly speaking the Borough heritage line moved to Trafford prompting a brand new club to be formed in Chorley which eventually emerged into the Lynx. But the spiritual connection with Blackpool Borough remained and there would be plenty of people happy to see them return to the seaside (and preferably wear tangerine, black and white colours.)

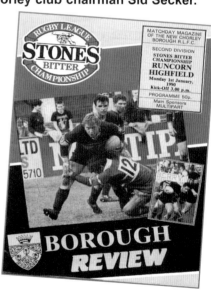

ANNUAL REPORT
2004

NOTHING else that happened in 2004 really mattered for Chorley Lynx when news emerged just before their final National League Two fixture of the season that the club faced closure after its financial backers decided to stop propping it up. It is impossible to keep a semi-pro Rugby League club alive on average crowds of less than 400 unless you have outside sources of income, and

the plug was being pulled on Chorley after several seasons of struggle. Sadly all this came at a time when the Lynx were a more than useful side on the field and had been galvanised by the personality of their coach in 2004,

Mark Lee. Emotions spilled over in their last match, against front-runners York, when Chorley's stand-off Brian Capewell produced a sensational last minute drop-goal from inisde his own half to secure a 21-20 victory at the aptly (on this occasion) named Victory Park. The Lynx finished in seventh place just missing a play-off position. Will they re-emerge somewhere else in Lancashire?

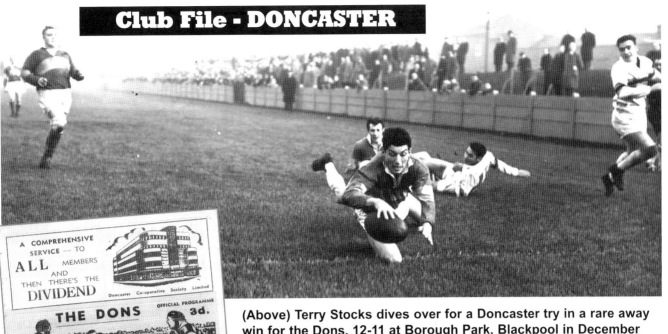

(Above) Terry Stocks dives over for a Doncaster try in a rare away win for the Dons, 12-11 at Borough Park, Blackpool in December 1963. It was Blackpool's first season at their new ground.

Some well known names like Les Belshaw, Dennis Hartley, Brian Wrigglesworth and Freddie Williamson on this Doncaster team at Tattersfield from the 1957-58 season. Left to right (Back row): Belshaw, Hartley, Baddeley, Hayter, Matthews, Shoebottom, Hinchliffe. (Front row): Worsely, Stokes, Wrigglesworth, Wilkinson, Northern, Williamson and Ratcliffe.

ANNUAL REPORT
2004

DONCASTER are looking to a bigger and brighter future when they get their promised new stadium, and much emphasis at the club is being put on development officers being funded to encourage more youngsters to learn the game. Doncaster's chairman John Wright has made no secret of his wish for the club to make it up into the Super League, but 2004 probably illustrated just how much work needs to be done before that can be approached. With crowds in hundreds and a team that played very much in the image of its coach St.John Ellis, Doncaster finished in sixth place in National League One, before being knocked out in the first round of the play-offs 63-22 at Hull K.R.

It is 25 years since Yorkshire Television made its much acclaimed documentary about the trials and tribulations of Doncaster Rugby League Club *"Another Bloody Sunday."* That summed up the struggles of a club which had rarely been too far away from the bottom of the league apart from its excellent debut season in 1951-52. But an altogether different anniversary in 2004 was that it was exactly ten years since Doncaster were sitting pretty at the very top of the elite division. The newly promoted Dons made a stunning entry to their life in Division One at the start of the 1994-95 season, winning away at St.Helens and then beating Widnes at home to leave them top of the table. A record Tattersfield crowd of 6,017 gathered to see Doncaster's second home match of the season against Leeds, which was also televised live by Sky. Leeds won a close game 16-6 and that was a good as it got for the Dons before financial problems became apparent. In their team back then were Jamie Bloem, Vila Matautia and Audley Pennant.

The inimitable Mike Stephenson proudly holds the Championship trophy aloft after leading Dewsbury to one of the most famous achievements in their long and illustrious history. Dewsbury were crowned Champions of the Rugby League in May 1973 after out-foxing Leeds in the Final at Odsal Stadium.

ANNUAL REPORT
2004

IF there's one club guaranteed to improve in 2005 it's going to be Dewsbury. Because things could not get much worse for the Rams than they were in 2004 in which they finished next to bottom of National League Two with only Gateshead below them. As expected, relegation to the lower division proved to be a disaster for Dewsbury - with their playing resources stripped bare they managed to win only three League games and suffered the indignity of being knocked out of the Challenge Cup by amateurs Sharlston.

So, the only way is up and Dewsbury have every confidence that having got relegation out of their system they can now start rebuilding with experienced coach Andy Kelly at the helm. In 2004 they had an outstanding player in full-back Wayne McHugh and a regular points scorer in scrum-half Adam Thaler.

There must be something in the water in Dewsbury that helps create high-profile television commentators for Rugby League. The British game's biggest t.v. personality for over 30 years was Eddie Waring, a mantle that has now been inherited by Mike Stephenson - and both hailed from the town in the Heavy Woollen district of Yorkshire. Dewsbury boys who made good, Eddie as a team manager, promotor and journalist, "Stevo" as a player who captained his home town team to a famous triumph to be crowned R.L. Champions in 1972-73, a season in which he had also played a key role in Great Britain's World Cup win. As a player he brought a new dimension to the role of the hooker in open play, and set a new world record transfer fee when he left Dewsbury to join the Australian club Penrith, where his career in the media first took shape.

42

Memorabilia which recalls another Championship Final for Dewsbury - this one in 1947 against Wigan at Manchester's Maine Road. The autographs on this programme include those of Dewsbury heroes like Charlie Seeling and Vic Hey, as well as Gus Risman, and in the Dewsbury team Jimmy Ledgard, Harry Royal and Harry Hammond.

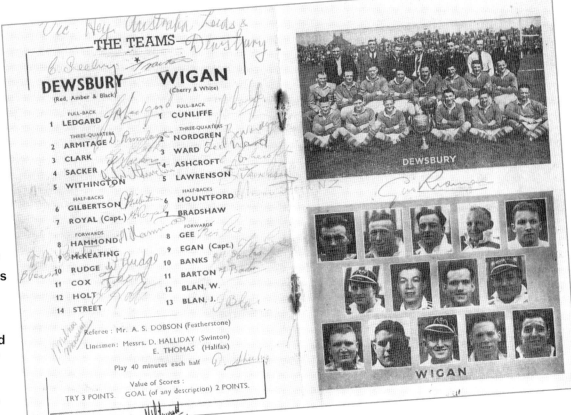

Whilst "Stevo" led Dewsbury to what was probably the greatest day in their history on 19 May 1973, when they beat Leeds 22-13 in the Championship Final at Odsal Stadium, remember the club were no strangers to glory days having won the Challenge Cup in 1912 and then having the honour of playing in the very first Final staged at Wembley in 1929. They also were runners-up in the 1947 Championship Final against Wigan (see programme above) at a time when great Dewsbury players like Jimmy Ledgard, Harry Royal, Harry Hammond and Harry Street were playing at Crown Flatt. And during the emergency days of World War Two, the enterprise of Eddie Waring saw Dewsbury parade a team of stars which took them to three successive Championship Finals and a Challenge Cup Final. Modern times saw Dewsbury win the 2000 Northern Ford Premiership title, with their former hooker Neil Kelly as coach and stars players like Nathan Graham and Barry Eaton, only to be denied promotion to the Super League.

The 1973 Championship Final as Dewsbury's Nigel Stephenson has Leeds on the run at Odsal with big Jeff Grayshon up in support.

Whilst Dewsbury will always remember the men who took their team to Cup Finals and Championships in the past, in more modern times the old Crown Flatt ground saw many fine players who wore the red, amber and black hoops with such distinction. None better than stand-off CHRIS VASEY (above) who joined Dewsbury in 1982 from local amateurs St.John Fisher and became one of their stars. Eventually Chris was signed by Leeds in the 1988-89 season for a record transfer-fee for the Dewsbury club - his move to Headingley effectively enabled Dewsbury to finance recruting several new players including half-backs Chris Wilkinson and Willie Johnson, centre Gary Moore and experienced former Leeds and Hull forward John Carroll.

Unmistakably Featherstone Rovers - this team pictured before playing Hull K.R. in a battle of the Rovers at Craven Park in October 1962, Left to right (Standing): Colin Clift, Vic Rawes, Tony Lynch, Dave Lamming, Norman Hockley, Eric Broom, Les Hammill. (In front): Ivor Lingard, Carl Dooler, Joe Mullaney (Captain), Jack Fennell, Ken Greatorex and Walter Ward.

ANNUAL REPORT
2004

FEATHERSTONE Rovers finished the 2004 season on a high with a fine run in the National League One play-offs after finishing in fifth place. Rovers went away to both Oldham and Hull K.R. and won, before finally going out at Whitehaven in the final eliminator before the Grand Final. It was enough to give plenty of cause for optimism for next year for Featherstone who gave a chance to a rookie coach in Gary Price and found him to be quite a breath of fresh air.

Rovers season in 2004 really turned for the better following the arrival of French scrum-half Maxime Greseque at Post Office Road. His passing and kicking skills gave the side a new dimension and he quickly became a big favourite with the Featherstone fans. Up front, Rovers had good solid forwards throughout the year in Ian Tonks, Stuart Dickens and Jimmy Carlton.

It's hard to break the ties that bind and Featherstone Rovers have always been one of the strongest examples you could find of a Rugby League club being the centre of its community. Things are different now the pits have closed but Rovers still carry the family links through the generations and it was reassuring to see a Tonks, a Newlove and a Dooler in their team in 2004. It's a very similar situation in the small communities which support Rugby League clubs in France and Featherstone got first hand appreciation of that this year when they welcomed Maxime Greseque, son of the former French Test scrum-half Ivan Greseque. For a place with such a small population Featherstone's achievements in Rugby League have been incredible, with three Challenge Cups and a Championship to their name, plus the production of no less than 16 Great Britain players.

David Hobbs lifts the Cup the last time Featherstone won at Wembley, beating Hull in 1983.

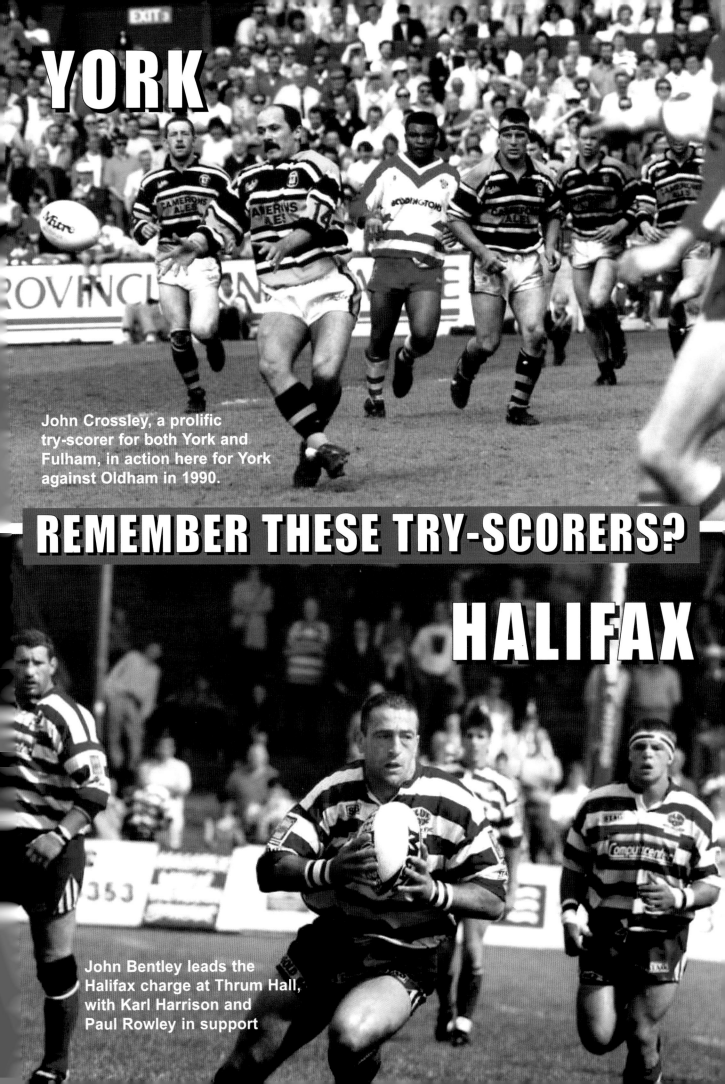

YORK

John Crossley, a prolific try-scorer for both York and Fulham, in action here for York against Oldham in 1990.

REMEMBER THESE TRY-SCORERS?

HALIFAX

John Bentley leads the Halifax charge at Thrum Hall, with Karl Harrison and Paul Rowley in support

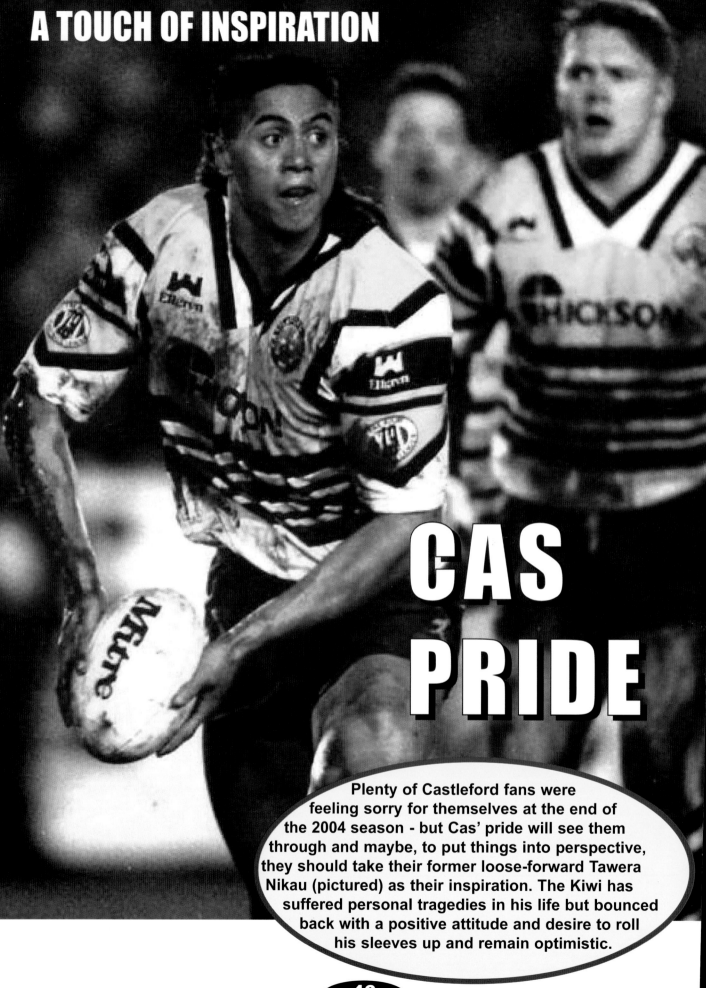

CAS PRIDE

Plenty of Castleford fans were feeling sorry for themselves at the end of the 2004 season - but Cas' pride will see them through and maybe, to put things into perspective, they should take their former loose-forward Tawera Nikau (pictured) as their inspiration. The Kiwi has suffered personal tragedies in his life but bounced back with a positive attitude and desire to roll his sleeves up and remain optimistic.

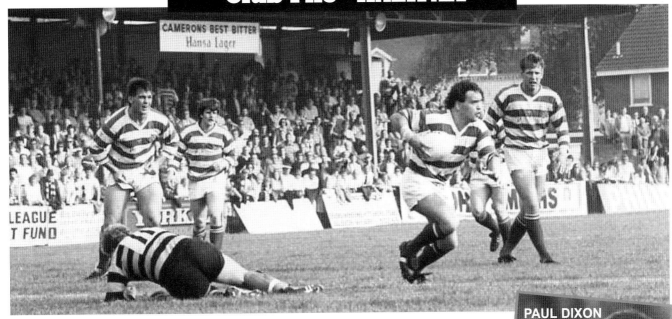

Flashback to the famous blue and white hoops of Halifax in their era of success led by Chris Anderson in the late 1980s. Here, scrum-half Gary Stephens has the ball with forwards Cavill Heugh, Paul Dixon and Neil James in support.

PAUL DIXON in his G.B. days

History may come to judge that incredible five minute spell in the 2004 play-off final against York as a crucial moment in the life of Halifax Rugby League Club. Had they gone down to National League Two the downward spiral may well have taken them into oblivion. Instead, they have a second chance to start rebuilding a club with a wonderful history of achievement. The "boom and bust" scenario is nothing new, it happened after the Championship and Cup winning seasons in the late 'eighties, but now Halifax know the future has to be built on firm foundations, and with much respected former players like Paul Dixon and Mick Scott at the club, the qualities of hard work and honest endeavour will be the way ahead.

ANNUAL REPORT
2004

HALIFAX got a harsh lesson in reality in 2004. Many people in Rugby League seemed to assume that a team dropping down from Super League would automatically be front-runners in National League One. But that wasn't the case as Halifax, struggling for quality players, went into freefall. Fortunately for them, Anthony Farrell as player coach managed to stem the flow towards the end of the season, but they still needed an incredible five-minute purple patch at the end of the play-off final against York to avoid a second successive relegation and the loss of their Division One status - it was that close!

A moment Halifax will never forget as player-coach Chris Anderson lifts the Challenge Cup at Wembley in 1987. On the left is the Halifax chairman David Brook whilst on the right behind Anderson, RFL secretary-general David Oxley assists Prince Philip in presenting the plinth to Halifax second-rower Mick Scott.

The "Airlie Birds" in 1959, the first year they went to Wembley. Left to right (Standing): Brian Saville, Brian Cooper, Cyril Sykes, Bill Drake, Jim Drake, Arthur Keegan. (Seated): Brian Hambling, Johnny Whiteley, Mick Scott, Stan Cowan, Tom Finn. (In front): R. Boustead, George Matthews. (Inset photos): Tommy Harris, Peter Whiteley and Ivor Watts.

ANNUAL REPORT
2004

ON the surface 2004 was a year in which Hull were very successful as they broke up the so-called "big four" of Super League by finishing in third place ahead of both Wigan and St.Helens. But they were unable to make home field advantage pay in the play-offs as, missing several key players with injuries, they were knocked out by Wakefield Trinity. The shine of what should have been a successful season was further damaged at the end by reports of a £2 million debt and supporter unrest over price increases. Hull will desperately miss Shaun McRae in 2005 and with injury hit veteran stars like Jason Smith and Richie Barnett also gone, much will rest on the impact new boy Stephen Kearney can have alongside the outstanding Richard Swain and half-back Richard Horne. 2004 was a very good year, but for a lot of Hull supporters, you're only as good as your last game

With an average of 11,458 at their new K.C. Stadium, Hull were the fourth best supported club in Super League in 2004, yet when they played cross-city rivals Hull K.R. in a pre-season friendly in early January a remarkable crowd of almost 16,000 turned out to see it. It wasn't summer and it wasn't Super League, it wasn't even a competitive fixture, yet all those people wanted to see the black and whites play the red and whites in a Hull derby again. If that wasn't a loud and clear message about what really makes Rugby League tick, nothing could be.

(Above) Steve Norton, one of the greats to wear the famous black and white number 13 shirt, just like Johnny Whiteley before him.

The Robins who flew to Wembley for the first time in 1964. Left to right (Standing): Cyril Kellett, Eric Palmer, Len Clark, Brian Tyson, John Moore, Mike Blackmore, Terry Major, John Taylor. (In front): Alan Burwell, Peter Flanagan, Harry Poole (Captain), Graham Paul and David Elliott.

ANNUAL REPORT
2004

HULL Kingston Rovers made a big impact on the media before the 2004 season started with their high profile coaching and management trio of Martin Hall, Malcolm Reilly and Nick Halafihi. But by the end of the season all three had left Craven Park and the Robins were back to the drawing board. For a club with such a great pedigree as Rovers and in a city that would thrive on having both its clubs back in the elite, 2004 was seen as an excellent opportunity to win promotion to Super League with no full-time Huddersfield or Salford to contend with this year. It wasn't to be for a Rovers side who disappointed on several occasions. They finished third in National League One, well behind Leigh and Whitehaven, and were knocked out of the play-offs at home to Featherstone. Earlier in the year Hull K.R. had made the Arriva Trains Cup Final only to be heavily beaten in it by Leigh. Kiwi Paul Mansson and former East Leeds half-back Phil Hasty were among Rovers best along with big Papua New Guinean prop Makali Aizue.

The club from East Hull were pioneers in the British game at a time when top coaching brains like Colin Hutton and Roger Millward were eager to adapt the best ideas from the Australian game to their team at Craven Park. Although it took a touch of Kiwi magic to help Rovers to their Championships in the 1980s with Gary Prohm, Gordon Smith and Mark Broadhurst key men with David Hall and Mike Smith.

Hull K.R.'s David Hall lifts the Premiership trophy in 1985 when the Robins ruled the roost in Rugby League.

Do you recognise the tall fellow in the middle of the back row of this Fartown team in 1972-73? It's Wayne Bennett, long-time mentor of the Brisbane Broncos and currently coach of the Australian national team. The players are, left to right (Back row): Stephen Shaw, Dave Weavill, David Wroe, Greg Veivers, Wayne Bennett, Bob Tomlinson, Graham Naylor, Frank Davies, Malcolm Branch. (Front row): Chris Leese, Trevor Bedford, John Drury, Kenny Loxton, Trevor Doyle and Ken Senior.

HUDDERSFIELD CRICKET AND ATHLETIC CLUB FOOTBALL PROGRAMME

— OFFICIAL —

laret and gold, Fartown, the George Hotel... Huddersfield is a place steeped in Rugby League history. From the distant days in the early part of the 20th Century when the legendary Harold Wagstaff led the "Team of All Talents" through to the decade after World War Two when Huddersfield were the great entertainers of the game with a side featuring Aussie stars Lionel Cooper and Pat Devery, Scotsman Dave Valentine, Welshman Billy Banks and Cumbrians Bob Nicholson, Jeff Bawden and Russell Pepperell, Fartown was the scene of some of the game's finest football. Tommy Smales continued that tradition when he captained to Huddersfield to the Championship and a Wembley Final in 1962 with a team containing favourites like "Spanky" Dyson, Peter Ramsden and Don Close.

Fartown heroes Tommy Smales and "Spanky" Dyson enjoy the moment in 1962 when Huddersfield were crowned Champions of the Rugby League.

ANNUAL REPORT
2004

HUDDERSFIELD had very high hopes during the first part of the 2004 season with the very real prospect of a top six place and, even more exciting, a first Challenge Cup Final since 1962. Their Cup hopes fell apart in the face of a St.Helens onslaught in the semi-final and some inconsistent form in the second half of the League campaign saw them slip away out of the play-offs into seventh position. Mind you, a few short years ago such high levels of achievement would have seemed just a dream for Huddersfield, so it's a measure of the progress made under Jon Sharp in 2004. They said goodbye to outstanding players Brandon Costin and Darren Fleary at the end of the season.

The Parkside boys of 1965 - this was the Hunslet squad which etched their names into Wembley history by putting on a wonderful show against Wigan. Left to right: (Back row) C.Taylor, Geoff Gunney, Alan Marchant, Bernard Prior. (Middle row) John Griffiths, Bill Ramsey, Dennis Hartley, Ken Eyre, Arthur Render, Billy Baldwinson. (Seated) Barry Lee, Billy Langton, Fred Ward (captain-coach), Geoff Shelton, Alan Preece. (In front) Brian Gabbitas and Ray Abbey.

Hunslet's reputation as a great talent producing area for Rugby League was never better illustrated than their 1965 team which took part in that year's Wembley Cup Final against Wigan. Of their thirteen men who played in that memorable Final, no less than twelve were Yorkshiremen and nine of them were former Hunslet Juniors who learned the game in the Hunslet schools before graduating to Parkside.

The odd man out was big Welsh winger John Griffiths who had come north to join Hunslet from Pontypool Rugby Union club as a 19-year-old. The three non-Hunslet lads were captain-coach Fred Ward, scrum-half Alan Marchant and prop Dennis Hartley who came from as far away as Castleford, Featherstone and Hemsworth, respectively. The nine former Hunslet Juniors were: full-back Billy Langton; centres Geoff Shelton and Alan Preece; winger Barry Lee; stand-off Brian Gabbitas; hooker Bernard Prior; prop Ken Eyre; and second-rowers Bill Ramsey and Geoff Gunney.

Of those, Shelton, Gabbitas, Prior, Ramsey and Gunney were all Great Britain internationals, and it must be hard for young fans in 2004 to believe that one of the leading clubs in the game - as Hunslet were - could build their success so strongly on local junior products. No Australians, no New Zealanders, and of their three "imports" Marchant was signed from Halifax, Hartley from Doncaster and Fred Ward from York after a career that began for his home town Castleford and also took him to Leeds and Keighley. Those were happy times at Parkside.

ANNUAL REPORT
2004

HUNSLET got their year off to a good start with a revival of the pre-season Lazenby Cup taking a Leeds side south of the river and packing the South Leeds Stadium. That sight must have gladdened the heart of Hunslet chairman Graham Liles who decided to step down at the end of the 2004 season after 15 years at the helm, during which he pumped large amounts of money into keeping the club alive. On the field Hunslet battled on in National League Two with former player Roy Sampson still in charge of coaching and managed to win a play-off place by finishing sixth.

They then caused quite a surprise by travelling to Sheffield and knocking out the third placed Eagles. Hunslet's reward for that was another trip, to Workington, where their season came to an end with a 27-13 defeat. The little Kiwi general, Latham Tawhai, was back to guide Hunslet around the field in 2004, reviving memories of how he inspired them to their NFP Championship Grand Final win back in 1999. They also had solid seasons from props Danny Fearon and long-serving Mick Coyle and second-rower Wayne Freeman.

Lawkholme Lane 1974 - and how many of this Keighley team can you recognise? Among them: Dave Jickells, Paul Sutcliffe, Dave Garbett, John Burke, Dave Wilmot, Kenny Loxton, John Stephenson, Brian Jefferson, Derek Edwards (ex-Castleford), Peter Roe (Barrow coach in 2004) and Dean Raistrick.

ANNUAL REPORT 2004

Promotion to National League One proved to be too big a jump for the Keighley Cougars and they ended the 2004 season with just one win from 18 games and immediate relegation back to League Two. Whilst the Cougars will be confident they can rebuild in the lower division in 2005, their coach Gary Moorby knows they will have to do it without out-standing hooker Simeon Hoyle and prop Danny Ekis, who are both heading for Australia.

Brights spots in 2004 were centre Matt Foster finishing as League One's top try-scorer, the skills of Cumbrian Craig McDowall and the 100 per cent effort of loyal clubman Phil Stephenson.

Keighley followers can hardly fail to look back on the last decade and ask the question "what might have been?" Because it was in the 1994-95 season that they won the Championship of Division Two and "Cougar mania" hit its peak. All seemed set fare for Keighley to achieve the ambition they had worked long and hard to achieve and ascend into the elite division of the game. Then along came Super League and the Cougars were shut out. Their promotion was denied, the club went into financial freefall, Leeds signed their best play-ers and their coach at the time, Phil Larder, has gone on to be a guru of the England Rugby Union World Cup winners. For the club who pioneered the "razzmatazz" and community effort that became part of the Super League blueprint just up the road at Bradford, the irony of it all could not be stronger.

Full-back Brian Jefferson, the man who scored more points than any other in the history of the Keighley club. He played for England in 1968.

Fulham in their early days with some of the Londoners' favourite names. Left to right (Standing): Sean Hoare, David Allen, Harry Beverley, Joe Doherty, Charlie Jones, John Wood, Steve Mills, Roy Lester. (In front): Dave Eckersley, John Crossley, Tony Gourley, Reg Bowden, Steve Diamond, Tony Kinsey and Hussain M'Barki.

It was ten years this year since London became the Broncos, after the old London Crusaders were taken over by a Brisbane Broncos outfit who in 1994 obviously knew the proposed Super League was on the way. But for many, the fondest memories of London's professional club remain of the days when they were Fulham, playing in that distinctive all black kit with the white and red vees. The day Fulham first launched Rugby League at Craven Cottage in September 1980 - beating Wigan 24-5 - is remembered as one of the magical moments in the story of the game. With player-coach Reg Bowden prompting his juggernaut pack, which included Fulham hero Ian Van Bellen, the Londoners kicked off in fine style. Almost a quarter of a century later they are still here, albeit with a different name, playing in a different place in different colours, and playing what is virtually a different game - and still feeling like missionaries trying to spread an alien sport in the capital city. One of the biggest changes in recent years has been the huge increase in Rugby League development activity in the south east, encouraging youngsters to play the game. It's a far cry from the days when the stalwarts of the London Amateur League like Gordon Anderton, Mick Smyth and Dave Part flew the flag almost single-handed for developing the game in the capital. Hopes must be high now that all the investment is starting to create the long-awaited production line of genuine southern produced Rugby League players. London Broncos look forward to that - especially if the locals can turn up a few like Van Bellen, Roy Lester, Tony Gourley, Harry Beverley, Hussain M'Barki, or the other Fulham favourites.

Andrew Mighty, pictured above playing for South London in a London Amateur League Cup Final at Chiswick in 1988, was one of the original bright young products from the capital. He had first been featured in *"Open Rugby"* as a schoolboy in the original Peckham Pumas and went on to play for Hull F.C. under the coaching of Brian Smith.

ANNUAL REPORT
2004

LONDON Broncos flirted with the possibility of relegation in 2004, but came good with some vital wins at the back end of the season to preserve their Super League status. For the first time since they became the Broncos, the London side had as many, and sometimes more, English players than Australians - but it was still the brilliance of Dennis Moran which provided most of their match-winning quality. In 2005, coach Tony Rea will have to build a side without two of its mainstays, Jim Dymock and Steele Retchless, who retired at the end of this season. Playing at Brentford in west London the Broncos reported the lowest average crowd in the Super League at 3,458.

Leeds in the 1970-71 season. Left to right (back row): Bob Haigh, Phil Cookson, Les Dyl, John Holmes, John Burke, Tony Fisher, Ted Barnard, David Hick, John Atkinson. (front row): Mick Shoebottom, Alan Smith, Ron Cowan, Syd Hynes, Barry Seabourne (capt.), Tony Wainwright, Ray Batten and Bill Ramsey.

ANNUAL REPORT
2004

IT was a wonderful year for Rugby League at Leeds as they finished fully nine points ahead of all their Super League rivals and saw Headingley attendances soar to an average of over 16,000 with the house-full signs up at over 21,000 everytime local rivals Bradford came to play. Heady days indeed for a Leeds team that blossomed under the guidance of new coach Tony Smith - none better than captain Kevin Sinfield, young full-back Richie Mathers and try-scoring stand-off Danny McGuire. Exciting new additions in 2004 were winger Marcus Bai and forward Ali Lauitiiti. And with such a great youth development system in place the future looks very bright for Leeds.

Memories of Leeds at Wembley in 1978 with loose-forward Mick Crane in possession watched closely by Phil Cookson and John Holmes. Crane, better known as a Hull F.C. player, was a magical ball-handler and the antidote to the modern world of full-time training and hard yards.

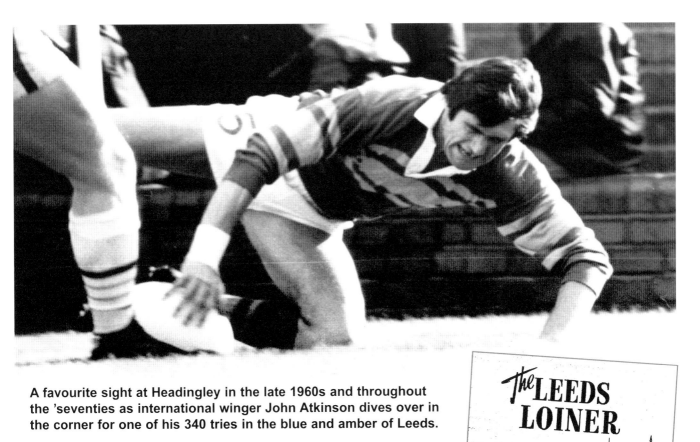

A favourite sight at Headingley in the late 1960s and throughout the 'seventies as international winger John Atkinson dives over in the corner for one of his 340 tries in the blue and amber of Leeds.

Elsewhere in this *"Rugby League Journal Annual"* you can read about Danny McGuire following in the footsteps of such great local Leeds lads like John Holmes and Mick Shoebottom filling the stand-off role at Headingley with such success - and it is always reassuring to see the traditional talent producing areas of Amateur Rugby League continuing to provide the platform for success at a club that has always been seen as a glamourous magnet for overseas stars. The modern world of Super League is no different to years gone by in that respect and Leeds in 2004 owed much of their success to the platform provided up front by two players from the Heavy Woollen area - hooker Matt Diskin and prop Danny Ward. Likewise the half-backs Danny McGuire and Rob Burrow and the emerging full-back Richie Mathers. Captain Kevin Sinfield was a very successful English Schools international who learned his rugby with BARLA club Waterhead in his home town of Oldham. Such links continue with no less than five of the nine Leeds players in this year's successful Great Britain Academy team being produced by the Drighlington Amateur club. It was always the same in the great Leeds Championship winning teams of the 1960s guided by Joe Warham and then Roy Francis and the double Wembley winners of the 'seventies when Syd Hynes was coach. Stars aplenty have been brought in by Leeds, but the names of Yorkshire lads like John Holmes, Graham Eccles, Les Dyl, Steve Pitchford and David Ward will always be revered.

The Loiners hoist skipper David Ward and coach Syd Hynes aloft at Wembley in 1978. Also pictured: Willie Oulton, Les Dyl, John Atkinson, David Smith, Sammy Sanderson and Neil Hague.

This was Leigh in 1975 and now you know where Geoff got the idea about wearing a wig! They are, Left to right (Standing): Alan Rowley, Dave Macko, Eric Hughes, Clive Jones, D.Wheeler, Keith Fairbrother, John Davies, Alan Riding. (In front): Mick Pythian, Mick Stacey, Mick Hogan, Geoff Fletcher, John McAtee, Cliff Sayer and Joe Walsh.

ANNUAL REPORT
2004

LEIGH finally got where they wanted to be after winning promotion to Super League as National League One champions in 2004. But they were just a couple of minutes away from missing out again in a Grand Final against Whitehaven which Leigh only managed to send into extra- time with a late Neil Turley drop-goal. But, after missing out so many times in previous years, Leigh weren't worried about how they won or whether they were gracious in victory or not. It was a fairytale return for home-town boy Tommy Martyn in the Grand Final that took Leigh into Super League, and throughout the season they had out-standing players in full-back Neil Turley and for-wards like David Larder and Simon Knox. To cap a season of success for the side coached by Darren Abram, Leigh also won the Arriva Trains Cup and the League Leaders' trophy. Now for life with the Super League big boys.

For a club that has lived in the shadow of its big-brother neighbours like Wigan, Warrington and St.Helens, Leigh's record in Rugby League is a proud one. Their most recent major achievements were winning the Challenge Cup in 1971 inspired by Alex Murphy and the Championship in

Leigh were Rugby League Champions of 1981-82, (above) Ray Tabern and Ian Potter hold the trophy.

1982. Now Leigh have finally won a place in the Super League it will be fasci-nating to see how a small-town club - but one so steeped in the game and a stronghold of Amateur Rugby League - will be able to compete in the elite. They have plenty of great players and achievements to inspire them.

Leigh - BBC Floodlit trophy winners in 1972 with Tommy Martyn (senior) at the centre of the group and coach Les Pearce (far right.)

This was the Oldham team in 1964 under player-coach Frank Dyson. Left to right (Standing): Len McIntyre, Dave parker, Alf Mumberson, Charlie Bott, Ken Wilson, Harry Major. (Seated): Malcolm Price, Vince Nestor, Geoff Sims, Frank Dyson, Jim McCormack, John Donovan. (In front): Jack Pycroft.

Oldham still carry the tag as one the best teams never to have played at Wembley. For years it became something of a "Holy Grail" for Oldham people - despite the club taking part in no less than seven Challenge Cup Finals (including winning the Cup on three occasions) they were all in the early days before the Final was taken to Wembley and developed into such a showpiece occasion. Missing out on the game's highest profile occasion was particularly hard to take during the 1950s when Oldham were the great entertainers of Rugby League and consistently one of the game's most powerful teams.

JOHNNY NOON - one of the Oldham fans' favourites in years gone by. A local lad, he played 255 first-team games in the ten years from 1954 to 1964 for the "Roughyeds," before leaving to captain Rochdale Hornets.

Derek Turner, the captain of that great Oldham side, once recalled "We would have turned Wembley inside out and back again - but the harder we tried to get there, the worse our luck seemed to go. When I left Oldham and ultimately captained Wakefield on three occasions at Wembley, it only served to remind me of what might have been had the Oldham side of the 'fifties graced that sacred turf." Some consolation for Turner and that fine team was winning the Rugby League Championship in the 1956-57 season. They took the title after a 15-14 win over Hull in the Final played at Odsal Stadium in front of a crowd of 62,000 people. Star players in that team included scrum-half Frank Pitchford, powerful centre Alan Davies, try-scoring wingers Dick Cracknell and John Etty, goal-kicking full-back Bernard Ganley and mighty forwards like Charlie Winslade and Sid Little. Those names will always be associated with great times for Oldham.

ANNUAL REPORT
2004

OLDHAM won their customary play-off place to maintain their status as one of the leading clubs in National League One, but in the end 2004 went down as a disappointing campaign for the "Roughyeds." After finishing in fourth position in the table, Oldham were knocked out of the play-offs at home by Featherstone Rovers. It left a feeling of underachievement around Boundary Park which was swiftly followed by the club's decision not to retain Steve Molloy as their coach for next season.

As player-coach, Molloy had led from the front, despite battling injuries. There were good contributions from forwards Martin McLoughlin, Lee Doran and Phil Farrell, and nobody could have given more blood, sweat and tears to the Oldham cause than local lad Keith Brennan. But it was all to no avail for a club that once again faced the problem of being "homeless" in the middle of the summer season when they were forced to play "home" games at venues as far away as Chorley and Blackpool. It was all a far cry from those passionate winter days at the 'sheddings.

This Rochdale team from 1972-1973 contained some very experienced players which helped Hornets achieve 11th position (out of 30) in the league that season. Left to right (Back row): Bill Sheffield, Kevin Flanagan, Stuart Whitehead, Albert Hillman, Alan Robinson, Peter Clarke, David Taylor. (Front row): Peter Gartland, Tom Brophy, Bill Holliday, Willie Aspinall, Noman Brelsford, John Hammond.

R ochdale Hornets role in creating some of the most attractive tales in Rugby League folklore was emphasised in one of the best sports books to be published this year. *"The Glory of their Times"* told the stories of coloured players in the British game, and two of the most fascinating chapters were those on Wally McArthur, the Australian Aboriginal sprint champion who joined Hornets in 1953; and on the Fijians who came to Rochdale in the 1960s - among them Joe Levula, Orisi Dawai, Laitia Ravouvou, Voate Drui, Apisia Toga and later Mike Ratu. They made Hornets the most talked about club in the game.

85

ROCHDALE HORNETS
FOOTBALL CLUB CO., LTD.
ATHLETIC GROUNDS ROCHDALE
TELEPHONE 48004

HORNETS
v.
LIVERPOOL CITY
Saturday, 22nd December, 1962

OFFICIAL PROGRAMME 3d

ANNUAL REPORT
2004

HATS off to Bobbie Goulding who led a minor miracle in turning round the fortunes of this grand old club in 2004. Rochdale almost fell apart at the end of the 2003 season, with financial debts and the predictable mass exodus of players. Coach Martin Hall went to Hull K.R. and Hornets Chairman Ray Taylor was left with pretty much a blank sheet of paper and an empty cupboard as the new season approached. That's when Goulding came on the scene, eager for an opportunity as a coach back in the professional game. Only four players joined

Bobbie at Hornets' first training session in December 2003 - Lee Birdseye, Chris Campbell, John Braddish and Tony Kirwan.

In the early weeks of the season Rochdale, struggling for numbers, suffered some big defeats, but Goulding's spirit remained undaunted. As player-coach he still managed to guide his new team around the field, and step by step performances improved to

the point where Hornets were winning games and giving some of the top sides in National League One a run for their money - with the highlight coming when they thrashed Leigh on their own ground. This revival meant that Rochdale, who seemed certain for relegation at the start of the season, avoided that and preserved their Division One status - eventually finishing just two more wins away from a play-off place. The future looks a lot better now for Rochdale Hornets - much better, for sure, than it did twelve months ago.

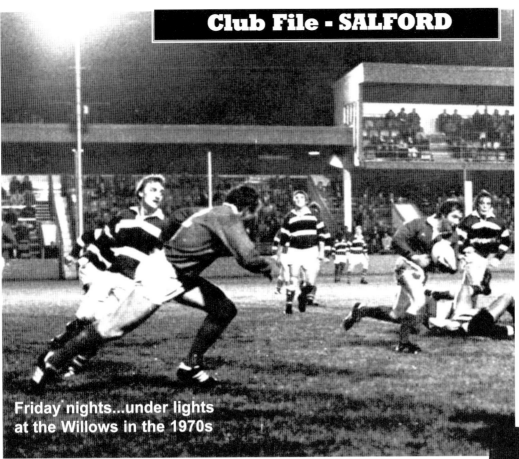

Friday nights...under lights at the Willows in the 1970s

In the 1970s Salford became synonymous with floodlit rugby. Friday nights at the Willows were a social highlight for the sporting public of the Manchester area as the Red Devils turned on the style through-out the winter. Pictured (left) we see Salford's stand-off Ken Gill on the attack under the glare of the lights with the flying wingman Keith Fielding in support - this match against Hunslet, who were known as New Hunslet at the time.

E lsewhere in this Annual you can read about the birth of the "Red Devils" nickname which was given to Salford on their pioneering tour to France seventy years ago in 1934. The original bearers of that famous name were the team put together, managed and coached by Lance Todd - and it was the dream of creating another golden era and another fabulous Salford team that inspired the late Brian Snape to build a set-up to try and emulate Toddy's origi-nal "Red Devils." Mr.Snape searched far and wide to bring the biggest stars to the Willows where he built an entertainments complex that became a focal point for the Manchester area. Rugby Union internationals like David Watkins, Mike Coulman, Maurice Richards and Keith Fielding mixed with great League thor-oughbreds like Bill Burgess, Paul Charlton, Colin Dixon and Steve Nash to pro-duce wonderful entertainment and success and Salford won two Rugby League Championship titles in 1974 and 1976.

SALFORD FOOTBALL CLUB

6^D

ANNUAL REPORT
2004

IN their first season back in the Super League following last year's promotion, Salford attained their first major goal - survival. The Reds finished the season in ninth position, with London, Widnes and Castleford below them. Their coach Karl Harrison was also elevated to the position of England coach. The Reds owed much to their departing scrum-half Gavin Clinch, who hung up his boots and was returning home to Australia at the end of the 2004 season. Clinch

got plenty of support from anoth-er Aussie, Kevin McGuiness and the New Zealander Cliff Beverley continued to play a key role in Salford's successes. Captained by hooker Malcolm Alker, the Reds had a big robust prop in Andy Coley, a player tipped for representative honours (shame there was no Lancashire county team this season) and likewise

for the versatile young back Karl Kirkpatrick.

Having maintained their Super League status, Salford are now pinning most of their hopes for future elevation on their pro-posed new stadium at Barton. Reports suggested the Reds would be as much as £2million a year richer from 2006 thanks to the casino development which is to be part of their new stadium. No wonder some player agents have been making a beeline for the Willows in anticipation!

St.Helens have become known as the great entertainers of Rugby League as well as being one of the most successful clubs of the modern era. Yet, although Saints played in the very first Challenge Cup Final way, way back in 1897, it was to be 1956 before they first got their hands on the coveted trophy. And whilst Saints have become famous for having some of the game's greatest players in their ranks - from Alan Prescott all the way through to Paul Sculthorpe today - their manager-coaches have also been among some of Rugby League's most interesting characters.

The master, of course, was Jim Sullivan who took over at Knowsley Road in 1952 and presided over seven years of unprecedented success - helping young players like Alex Murphy, Austin Rhodes and Vince Karalius become stars along the way. In the mid 1960s Saints broke the mould and stunned many people by appointing Joe Coan as coach. Joe hailed from Whitehaven and was a physical education teacher with no previous experience in Rugby League, yet he helped mould St.Helens into one of the most successful sides in their history. Alex Murphy, of course, had a four year spell as coach at Knowsley Road, and in more recent times Saints have also had such diverse figures as Kiwi Mike McClennan, Aussie Shaun McRae, one time Great Britain coach Ellery Hanley and now Ian Millward. Life is never boring for St.Helens.

ST. HELENS R.F.C.

Official Programme - Sixpence

Key figures in Saints' history of success, club chairman Mr. Harry Cook and captain Vince Karalius leading them out at Wembley in 1961.

ANNUAL REPORT
2004

SAINTS halo slipped a little in 2004 after their Easter Monday trip to Bradford came back to haunt them via the Sean Long-Martin Gleeson affair. Hefty suspensions to both was a blow for St.Helens and, whilst it appeared to be an incident blown out of all proportion by some sections of the media, it was the kind of publicity both their club and the game could have done without. As Saints finished in fifth place and went out of the play-offs at Wigan, controversy continued to follow them around as they were the victims of some desperately unfortunate video referee decisions.

That was the downside, the upside was another Challenge Cup triumph, this one made sweeter by beating old enemy Wigan in the Final at Cardiff. Plus the emergence of more young talents like James Roby, James Graham and Ian Hardman - and the 16 year-old English Schools international Scott Moore who became the youngest player ever to play in the Super League. Throughout the season Saints skipper Paul Sculthorpe led the way like the thoroughbred he is, always driving his team forward when injury forced the absence of both Cunningham and Higham.

This line-up from 1961-62 was one the best that Saints have ever seen. Left to right (Back row): Dick Huddart, Cliff Watson, Tom Van Vollenhoven, Abe Terry, Bob Dagnall, Don Vines. (Front row): John Donovan, Frank Barrow, Mick Sullivan, Vince Karalius, Alex Murphy, Wilf Smith and Brian McGinn.

Ray French has become one of St.Helens' best known natives as the BBC television Rugby League commentator for over 20 years and also a prolific writer and radio broadcaster. Ray has also been a major driving force behind the successful Saints ex-Players' Association and now the British Lions Association. Ray was an England Rugby Union international whilst still a student and joined his home town club at St.Helens in 1961. He gave Saints great service in the second-row. Later he joined Widnes in the deal that took Frank Myler to Knowsley Road and Ray enjoyed several good years with the Chemics, winning Great Britain Test honours in 1968 and playing in the World Cup down-under that year. *(Pictured above, right)* Ray French in his playing days for Saints in their 1966 Wembley win over Wigan - Ray is pictured getting a pass away to second-row colleague John Warlow. Having played with some of the greats at Knowsley Road including Alex Murphy, Vince Karalius, Dick Huddart, Austin Rhodes, Tom Van Vollenhoven and Tommy Bishop, Ray French is better place than anybody to judge who was the greatest of them all.

Tom Van Vollenhoven in classic style for Saints at Knowsley Road in the 1960s.

It was 2nd. September 1984 that Sheffield Eagles played their first game in the Rugby League, beating Rochdale Hornets 29-10 at the Owlerton Stadium. A crowd of 1,425 was there to see it. The Eagles were not quite the side their founder Gary Hetherington had hoped for before their initial prosposed sponsors went bust, but it didn't take long to make progress.

A picture from the Sheffield Eagles scrapbook as club founder Gary Hetherington prepares to lead the Eagles out alongside Swinton captain Alan Derbyshire in January 1985. This was in Sheffield's first season and the match was played at Bolton Wanderers' Burnden Park ground in the snow as Swinton's Station Road was frozen off.

ANNUAL REPORT
2004

SHEFFIELD Eagles might have have wished to have more to celebrate in a season which marked the 20th anniversary of the club's birth. In 2003 they had led the way in National League Two only to be denied promotion by losing the Grand Final to Keighley by the narrowest of decisions. It was a result that prompted the RFL to change the rules and ensure automatic promotion for the league leaders, which Barrow enjoyed in 2004.

This year the Eagles finished in third place and fell at the first hurdle of the play-offs, losing heavily at home to Hunslet in front of only 531 spectators. Coach Mark Aston, one of the survivors of the Eagles famous Wembley win, would have hoped for better in a season in which Sheffield always got great effort from big prop Jon Bruce and second-rower Andy Raleigh.

Within five years Sheffield had won their first significant trophy and won promotion to the First Division. The trophy came at Old Trafford as Daryl Powell (pictured right) the Eagles first signing and soon to become their first ever Great Britain international, led them to the Second Division premiership. But their greatest day came at Wembley in 1998 when Sheffield won the Challenge Cup. Remember the Eagles team that famous day: Waisale Sovatabua; Nick Pinkney, Whetu Taewa, Keith Senior, Matt Crowther; Dave Watson, Mark Aston; Paul Broadbent (capt.), Johnny Lawless, Dale Laughton, Paul Carr, Darren Shaw, Rod Doyle. Subs: Lynton Stott, Micahel Jackson, Darren Turner and Martin Wood.

GATESHEAD THUNDER

WITH just one win all season, the brave lads of Gateshead soldiered on. They finished bottom of National League Two but went mighty close to winning a few more. Local North East players like Kevin Neighbour, Steven Bradley and the Thorman brothers, Paul and Neil, were their backbone. Departing coach Seamus McCallion gave his all for a full season and in 2005, Gateshead's will re-commence their adventure with Dean Thomas as their new coach full of hope.

LONDON SKOLARS

LONDON'S second club in the professional ranks could look back on 2004, their second season in the League, with some satisfaction. A big impovement in their playing record got them six wins and a move up to third from bottom. Player coach New Zealander Alex Smits had a big Antipodean contingent led by loose-forward Mark Cantoni helping improve on field performances, whilst much good work continued off the field in promoting the game in north London.

Ghost-like memories of Station Road

The greying old picture above presents a ghost-like image of what used to be Swinton's home at Station Road. That wonderful arena in Manchester 27 which was the scene for some of the most famous moments in Rugby League history - Test matches, World Cup games, Championship Finals, Cup semi-finals and more, including such moments of Ashes folklore as the Chimpy Busch no-try Test in January 1930, Gasnier's hat-trick in 1959, the "massacre" of 1963 and the "ice bowl" decider of 1967. It was impossible to think of the Lions of Swinton without mention of Station Road and, despite the valiant efforts of those who have kept the Lions flag flying since, the club has never been the same since Station Road was sold in 1992 and they were forced to move out. They played out of Gigg Lane in Bury for almost a decade before the foundation of a Supporters' Trust prompted a move back closer to their roots. Swinton played at the ground of non-league Salford Football Club and in 2004 they moved to play at the home of Sedgeley Park Rugby Union club.

With crowds of just a few hundred, it's a long way from the days when Swinton were back-to-back Champions in the 1960s, and their star team boasted a theequarterline with the wonderfully named Speed and Fleet alongside internmationals Alan Buckley and Johnny Stopford. All with the rock-solid full-back Ken Gowers behind them.

ANNUAL REPORT
2004

SOME kind of mission accomplished for Swinton in 2004 as they rose to the higher echelons of National League Two to finish in fourth place. That gave them a home game in the play-offs which they lost in a high-scoring match with Workington Town. With a young coach, Paul Kidd, at the helm for his first season, there was plenty of satisfaction with results on the field for a once mighty club whose major battles in recent years have been for survival rather than championships or cups. The Lions, once again, had a real stand-out player in full-back Wayne English who has been consistently one of the best in the game over recent seasons. Other notable players included stand-off Mick Coates and back-rowers Ian Hodson and Rob Russell.

Johnny Stopford - try-scoring international winger in the famous Lions Championship winning threequarter line.

Trinity enjoy their third Challenge Cup in four years at Wembley in 1963 as captain Derek Turner is chaired by his jubilant team. (Left to right) Standing: Malcolm Sampson, Gerry Round, Keith Holliday, Turner, Jack Wilkinson, Roger Pearman, Ian Brooke, Milan Kosanovic, Paddy Armour (masseur), Brian Briggs. In front: Committe man, Ken Traill (coach), Gert Coetzer, Colin Greenwood, Don Vines, Harold Poynton, Neil Fox and Ken Hirst. Wakefield had just beaten Wigan in the Final to take the Cup.

ANNUAL REPORT
2004

THE name of Wakefield Trinity was back among the elite of Rugby League in 2004 after a great season which saw them attain sixth place and then beat Hull and run Wigan mighty close in the play-offs. With no less than eight Antipodeans in their starting X111 at Wigan in the last match of their campaign, the quality of Trinity's overseas recruitment has been a key to their improvement and they certainly were one of the most entertaining teams to watch in the Super League keeping the ball alive and backing up. It was all a credit to their Aussie coach Shane McNally. The new success saw Trinity's average crowds rise by 20% to 4,804.

Recruitment was the buzz word as Wakefield turned on the style so well in 2004 - with Australians like Jason Demetriou, Sid Domic, Ben Jeffries and Michael Korkidas being joined by Semi Tadulala and David Solomona in making Trinity such an excellent side to watch. Whilst so many Super League clubs now find their ranks similarly dominated by overseas players, it comes asa reminder that top English clubs have always scoured the world for new talent, although for many years the international transfer ban meant their targets had to be Rugby Union players. Wakefield were one of the clubs who became most associated with recruitment in South Africa, to the point where Trinity were the British club best known over there and invited to play a tour in South Africa in 1962. In the Wakefield team victorious at Wembley in 1963 (pictured above) were South African wingers Colin Greenwood and Gert Coetzer - and no Trinity fans of that era could ever forget the brilliant centre Alan Skene. Also in that 1963 team was Welsh forward Don Vines, who came to Wakefield via Oldham and St.Helens. Now, just as back then, local lads provided the perfect mix, and Trinity will be hoping their current captain Gareth Ellis, will go on to be just as successful as another powerfully built young centre representing his local club - a certain Neil Fox.

Flashback to Belle Vue on 10 December 1956 as the Australian touring team line up alongside Wakefield Trinity, including a teenager called Neil Fox. Trinity went on to beat the Aussies 17-12 in a fiery match.

The Wakefield Trinity players alongside club secretary Mr. G. Thomas (standing far left) are: Left to right (Back row): Holliday, Fox, Haigh, Fred Smith, Armstead, Chamberlain. (Middle row): Kelly, Shaw, Harrison. (In front): Rollin, Hirst, Wilkins and Bullock. The figures of Norm Provan and skipper Clive Churchill are easily identified on the Kangaroos' side of the picture, their full team that day was: Churchill; Adams, Payne, O'Brien, Moir; Johnston, Connell; Furner, Hammerton, Davies, Provan, Purcell and Marsh. As Trinity won 17-12, both Norm Provan and Wakefield's Joby Shaw were sent off, whilst three Aussies - Davies, Don Furner and Purcell - were carried off. It was quite a day at Belle Vue!

More Wembley memories for Trinity. (Above) at the first post-war Challenge Cup Final in 1946 as Wakefield captain Billy Stott introduces Trinity's Jim Croston to the Prime Minister Mr. Clement Attlee. Stott kicked a late penalty to give Wakefield a 13-12 win over Wigan. (Right) the South African winger Gert Coetzer dives over for a try in the 1963 Final as Trinity again beat Wigan at Wembley. Coetzer was in his first season of Rugby League when he won a Cup winners medal and became a massive favourite at Trinity.

Fifty years ago, this was the Warrington team which won the "double" in 1954. They are: Left to right (Standing): Eric Frodsham, L.Horton, H.Fishwick, A.Stevens, Gerald Lowe, Austin Heathwood, S.Phillips. (Seated): Frank Wright, Stan McCormick, Alistair Naughton (Captain), Harry Bath, Bob Ryan. (In front): Ray Price, Gerry Helme. (Insets): Jim Challinor and Brian Bevan.

There have been no shortage of significant 50th anniversaries to celebrate in 2004 which tells us that 1954 must have been quite a year. The first World Cup, the record crowd for the Cup Final replay at Odsal Stadium, the birth of Blackpool Borough, to mention just a few. And Warrington have their own big reason to celebrate because they won the coveted Cup and Championship "double" in 1954, beating Halifax in both Finals, one of which was the famous Odsal replay. It was a golden era for the "Wire" who had also won the Challenge Cup at Wembley in 1950 and were to retain the Championship title in 1954-55. In 1954 they went threequarters of the way to winning the legendary "All Four Cups" - a feat achieved by just three clubs in the history of the game: Hunslet, Huddersfield and Swinton. The one trophy Warrington missed in 1953-54 was the Lancashire Cup. Aussies Brian Bevan and Harry Bath were two of the biggest stars alongside British internationals like Gerry Helme, Stan McCormick and Alistair Naughton.

THERE seems little doubt that Warrington are a growing force again in Rugby League. Logic suggests that, because in the modern world of Super League cash is the key and Warrington now appear to be in a position to significantly increase their revenue streams - with a wealthy backer and the success of their new stadium in attracting bigger crowds - to where they can seriously rival the big four. A statement of intent for 2005 has already been laid down with the recruitment of players of the calibre of Martin Gleeson and Logan

ANNUAL REPORT
2004

Swann. But all that's for the future, for the moment Warrington were left to ponder on a disappointing season on the field in 2004 after their heorics in making the top-six play-offs the previous year. Coach Paul Cullen is a hard task-masker and he had reason to feel let down by several performances during the course of the season. Half-backs Lee Briers and Nathan Wood were the key to

most of Warrington's best moments, but to drop to eighth place was a big disappointment - much of their season summed up by a bizarre performance in the Challenge Cup semi-final in which Warrington dominated much of the game but proceded to gift a place in the Final to Wigan. Nevertheless, after farewelling Wilderspool, their new Halliwell Jones stadium was a massive success with average crowds going up by a staggering 41% to make Warrngton the fifth best supported club in Super League. That augers well for their future.

The WIRE of '82

Remember these young lads at Warrington in 1982? Left to right (Back row): John Peake, Tommy Gittins, Dave Chisnall, Andy Holbrook, John Bevan, John Fieldhouse, Bob Eccles, Steve Hesford, Ronnie Duane, John Whittaker, Derek Finnegan. (Front row): Rick Thackray, Mike Kelly, Paul Fellowes, Carl Webb, Kevin Ashcroft (coach), Ken Kelly, Paul Cullen, Paul Ford and Tommy Rawlinson.

Ken Kelly pictured leading the Warrington attack against Widnes at what looks like a vibrant Wilderspool in the late 1970s. Ken was a very classy stand-off who was a big favourite with supporters of the "Wire." He won two Test caps for Great Britain as a Warrington player, one versus the 1980 Kiwis and the second (his last international apperance) against the "Invincibles" in the 1982 Ashes series. Ken had won two earlier Test caps against France in 1972 whilst he was a St.Helens player but injury made him miss the World Cup in '72.

Flashback to the 1971-72 season and this Widnes side reached the final of the Lancashire Cup. Left to right: (Standing): Mal Aspey, Alan Walsh, George Nicholls, John Foran, K.Irwin, Dave Macko, Denis O'Neil. (In front): Denis Brown, Ray Dutton, John Warlow, Johnny Gaydon, Mick McLoughlin and Reg Bowden.

ANNUAL REPORT
2004

WIDNES breathed a big sigh of relief after their last match of the 2004 season at Hull, becuse it was only then that they knew for sure Castleford had finished last and Widnes had survived for another year in Super League. It was a close call in a season which saw Widnes sack their coach Neil Kelly when things were looking dicy, and eventually bring over former Kiwi and Wigan boss Frank Endacott to assist former full-back Stuart Spruce in the relegation dogfight. Among a large contingent of overseas players Widnes were reliant on the Australians Julian (Jules) O'Neill and Shane Millard for most of their guidance around the field, what they need to see is more locals like Stephen Myler, Paul Devlin and David Mills coming through and making an impact.

Different times, different eras, but always success for Widnes as mighty forwards like Vince Karalius and Kurt Sorensen led them to Challenge Cup and Championship. These old programmes tell a story of how things used to be at Naughton Park as the "Chemics" were consistently one of the top sides in the game. Widnes always had a great tradition of

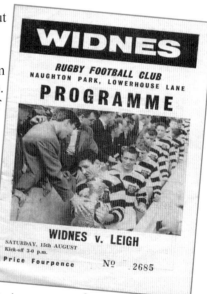

being a team of largely local lads. That changed in the 1980s when Doug Laughton recruited the likes of Sorensen, Koloto, Offiah, Tait and Jonathan Davies and they became the all-stars of Rugby League. But the locals were still there and, happily, some things don't change - in 2004 another young Myler was making his way in the team.

LEADING FROM THE FRONT

AARON LESTER

NATIONAL LEAGUE'S FINEST

FOR the past eight seasons **AARON LESTER** has been one of the most outstanding players in Britain outside the Super League. The publicity and the financial rewards that have come the way of many players of far lesser ability and determination have avoided the New Zealander who came from Auckland to join Whitehaven in 1997, but all those who have played against him - and most especially all the team-mates who have played alongside him - know that he has earned respect with a capital 'R.' Lester is a hooker/dummy-half as good as any, but more than that he has been a truly inspirational captain who always leads from the front. His toughness, durability and ability to play through the injury barrier have become legendary at Whitehaven, where his vital contribution to the club over recent years can never really be overstated. Aaron Lester is this Annual's choice as the National League player-of-the-year in 2004, just as he could have been over several of the past seven seasons. Also in the picture (above) taken in 2001 is **JASON RAMSHAW,** an equally fine servant to the Keighley Cougars and now doing fine work with the new York club.

WIGAN'S WEMBLEY CLASSICS

BRETT KENNY
1985 versus Hull

BILLY BOSTON

1965 versus Hunslet

Of all Wigan's 21 Challenge Cup Finals at Wembley none are more memorable than their victories over Hunslet in 1965 and Hull in 1985. Both were superb Finals, in which Hunslet and Hull played their full part before each lost by a narrow four-point margin. Who can forget the brilliance of Brett Kenny and John Ferguson in 1985 (see top picture) whilst below we see Billy Boston trying to evade Hunslet's Billy Langton at Wembley in 1965.

Wigan in 1959 and on their way to Wembley for a second consecutive year - nine local lads, two Welshmen, a South African and a Yorkshireman. Left to right (Standing): Billy Boston, Mick Sullivan, Fred Griffiths, Keith Holden, Eric Ashton (Captain). (Seated): Bill Bretherton, Bill Sayer, Norman Cherrington, Brian McTigue, John Barton, Roy Evans. (In front): Rees Thomas and David Bolton.

ANNUAL REPORT
2004

PROGRESSING as far as the final eliminator before the Grand Final officially made Wigan the third best team in Super League in 2004. In addition they got to the Challenge Cup Final - so in a season in which they were so badly hit by injuries and the loss of their first choice coach through illness, nobody at Wigan could complain that their team had been unsuccessful. Of course, some memories are still fresh of the years when Wigan used to win everything so people can be hard to please. Throughout 2004 it was hard to fathom the workings of the salary cap at Wigan, with bright young products like Robinson set to follow Briscoe and Johnson away from the JJB Stadium, but still talk of big import signings to replace such as Adrian Lam and Craig Smith. What was plain to see was just how much Wigan owed to their senior players Andrew Farrell and Kris Radlinski - both rose to new heights in leading from the front in 2004.

Wigan have always had a special relationship with Wembley since the day they played in the very first Rugby League Cup Final there way back in 1929. It will be a major target for the cherry and whites to be a part of the first Final back at the newly redeveloped Wembley stadium in 2006. Meanwhile 2005 provides two anniversaries of famous Wembley victories for Wigan - 40 years on from the 1965 Final with Hunslet and 20 years after the classic 1985 Final against Hull. Eric Ashton and Graeme West were the Wigan skippers who lifted the Cup on those two occasions.

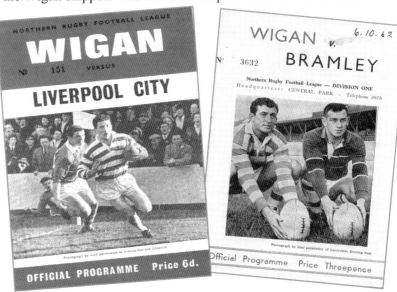

(Above) programme memories of times when even the little guys of Rugby League had their day at Central Park.

As Whitehaven fans basked in the warm glow of success in 2004, many cast their minds back to the events at the town's Civic Hall just four short years ago. That was when their demoralised club was about to have its death warrant signed, dressed up as a merger that would have taken them to Derwent Park, Workington. A handful of supporters were left angry, but powerless to stop it. But fortunately for Whitehaven - both the club and the whole town - there was one dissenting voice willing to speak from the stage of the Civic Hall and able to articulate a new

Whitehaven in 1965, left to right (Standing): Niah Vaughan, Dennis Williamson, Fred Hodgson, Charlie McCourt, Tom Hill, Matt McLeod. (In front): Alf Woolveridge, Alex Cassie, George Baker (Capt.), Barry Buchanan, Frank Snow, Phil Kitchin and Harry Maddison. Interesting points to note, four of the forwards (all local Cumbrians) - Vaughan, Hill, Williamson and McLeod - also played for Wakefield Trinity. A fifth, Charlie McCourt went on to play for Oldham and later died in a tragic accident working on the construction of the Channel tunnel. Niah Vaughan later became a successful round the world yachtsman.

way forward for the club. It involved supporters and club working together, setting a lead of voluntary effort, presenting a positive image in the media, winning back the respect of local Amateur clubs, businesses and potential

ANNUAL REPORT
2004

2004 will go down as a golden season for Whitehaven, a time when optimism touched new heights and the club finished the year literally just two minutes away from a place in the Super League. As well as reaching a major Final for the first time in the club's 56 year history, Haven's achievements were many. A 100% success record at home in the League, they had the player-of-the-year in Sam Obst and coach-of-the-year in Steve McCormack, plus were named as the RFL's official club -of-the-year. All this plus a home cup-tie versus Warrington live on BBC television - it was a time when all the hard work of the last three years came to fruition for a club that now has its community fully behind it.

sponsors, and taking an active role in community activites so that that community would realise just how much poorer it would be if its Rugby League club was taken away from it. The merger was stopped but it was to be a further 12 months before the direct action needed was taken to make the above start happening. The Whitehaven revolution began to take shape in the 2001-2002 season, with players and public responding positively to the new projects and new approach. Although the people who put it in place moved on, including then coach Paul Cullen who went to

Haven's all-time record try-scorer DAVID SEEDS has his achievement celebrated on this programme cover

Warrington, the hardest yards had been done and the good work has continued ever since with Steve McCormack a tremendously dedicated coach taking Whitehaven to new heights alongside high quality players like club captain Aaron Lester, David Seeds, David Fatialofa and Howard Hill playing with a commitment to the cause that has been inspirational.

2005 will see the 40th anniversary of Whitehaven's famous triumph over the 1965 New Zealand touring team. Haven won 12-7 that day and this picture shows centre John Coupe diving over for Whitehaven's first try as he outpaces Kiwis Roy "Fletcher" Christian and winger Pat White. On Coupe's elbow is stand-off Phil Kitchin, with Charlie McCourt and Alex Cassie coming up in support.

Tom Gainford was one of the unsung heroes of Whitehaven throughout the 1970s - a back-rower who played way above his weight, Tom signed on from Kells for £125 and went on to give eleven years service to Haven before they sold him to Barrow for a £9,000. Pretty good value for money!!! In the picture (above) Gainford is on the attack against Huyton with Geoff Fletcher moving in to tackle. Receration Ground buffs will also notice the roof on the "Popular Side" at that time - much missed but not forgotten.

(Above) VINCE GRIBBIN one of five Whitehaven G.B. Test caps.

Workington Town at the start of the 1962-63 season became the first winners of the Mackeson awards for high scoring - one of the first sightings of sponsorship in Rugby League - and also the Western Divisional championship. Here we see the Town team with their cup, which was actually the old Lancashire League trophy one of the original "All Four Cups," after being presented with Mackeson tankards by two representatives of Whitbreads, donors of the Mackeson awards. The Workington players are: left to right (Standing): Mick McFarlane, Dennis Martin, Ray Glastonbury, Rodney Smith, Matt McLeod, Frank Foster, John O'Neill. (In front): Syd Lowden, Harry Archer, Eddie Brenan, Brian Edgar, Sol Roper, Piet Pretorious.

ANNUAL REPORT
2004

WHEN New Zealander Ged Stokes arrived at Derwent Park to take over as coach for the 2004 season, he could hardly have taken on a bigger challenge. In the early part of the season Stokes's major challenge often appeared to be just finding enough lads to make up a team and the summit of Town's ambition became trying to avoid defeat against basement-dwellers Gateshead. But by the end of the campaign, everything had changed. Town had achieved fifth place in National League Two, they had beaten Swinton and Hunslet in the play-offs to go just one game away from their Grand Final, the public had started to support the club again and suddenly Workington Town had a future. Hope had returned to Derwent Park. Town's change in fortunes on the field was largely due to the abilities of new Kiwi signings Jonny Limmer and Lusi Sione and the returning Tane Manihera, plus the emerging talent of young forward Dean Burgess.

Fate can work in strange ways and the Rugby Football League will never be able to overstate the importance of their decision to open the tour of the New Zealand Residents team in Autumn 2003 with a match against Cumbria, because it may well have saved one of their most famous member clubs from extinction. Workington Town were in a desperate state as they looked ahead to 2004 - they had no coach, hardly any players and there was no sign of anyone in the British game capable of stepping in as a manager/coach and being able to tackle the massive odds Town were battling against to try and stop their downward spiral.

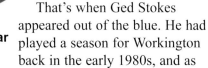

LUSI SIONE - Kiwi star at Workington Town.

That's when Ged Stokes appeared out of the blue. He had played a season for Workington back in the early 1980s, and as coach of the New Zealand Residents team he found himself being reaquainted with the area during the tourists' stay on the Cumbria coast before their opening fixture. He was also reaquainted with Dave Smith, a former team-mate at Workington and in 2003 Town's football director working

In 2005 it will be fifty years since Workington and Barrow met in the Challenge Cup Final - for Town it was their second Wembley Final in three years. Above (left) captain Billy Ivison is pictured leading the Workington team out alongside Barrow skipper Willie Horne and (right) Town's teenage scrum-half John "Sol" Roper shakes hands with the Duke of Edinburgh as the Workington team is introduced.

Souvenirs of Workington Town's incredible early achievements - (above) the programme for the 1952 Cup Final at Wembley and (right) the great Gus Risman tackled by Warrington's Gerry Helme in the 1951 Championship Final at Maine Road, Manchester.

overtime to try and find some way to turn the club's fortunes around. Stokes accepted the challenge that few would-be coaches in the British game were prepared to take on and it was a real coup for Workington Town to be getting the man who had effectively been the assistant coach of the full Kiwi national team for the last few years. And after months of struggling with a lack of players, during which time Town had to host Leeds in a Challenge Cup tie that created wonderful publicity and helped clear some debts, Stokes started to see some light at the end of the tunnel by recruiting three of his boys from New Zealand, Jonny Limmer, John Tuimaualuga and the maverick full-back Lusi Sione. In addition there was the return of Tane Manihera after his Rugby Union commitments were over and likewise Welsh forward Gareth Dean from Carcassonne in the French League. Plus Town discovered a gem when teenage forward Dean Burgess was released by Whitehaven and suddenly good local amateurs were prepared to sign for them again. It all augers well for 2005, a year in which Workington plan to celebrate the 60th anniversary of the club's foundation. It will also be 50 years since they played at Wembley in the 1955 Cup Final against Barrow.

Familiar faces in this York team circa 1980 at Clarence Street include: Derek Foster, Brendan White, Alan Rhodes, Billy Harris, Gary Smith, Terry Day, Kevin Harkin and John Crossley.

York's old ground at Clarence Street was one of the most pleasantly situated in the Rugby League, nestling in the shadow of the Minster, and it is good to see a revival in the profile of the game in the city with the success of the new Knights professional club and the establish-

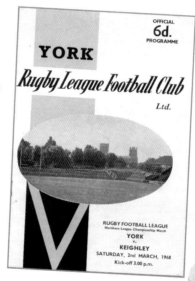

ment of the York Nines festival as annual event at the Heworth club that now brings visiting teams from far and wide. Despite the troubles of the old Wasps, York has remained a stronghold of Amateur Rugby League and

ANNUAL REPORT
2004

UNDER their new guise as the City Knights, York continued to make much positive progress in 2004 - their second season since the new club emerged. As the best supported club in National League Two they went agonisingly close to winning promotion - after finishing second to Barrow in the League, York won through to the play-off final and were just minutes away from beating Halifax. Fate stepped in and it wasn't to be, but York will continue to set the pace in 2005 with a new coach in Mick Cook aligned to a link up with Leeds. Coach Malcolm Agar is heading for Hull in 2005 but can reflect on a job well done, with two excellent half-backs in Scott Rhodes and Danny Brough and an experienced leader in Lee Jackson.

the City Knights have tapped into all that latent interest and enthusiasm. But the memories of the old days at Clarence Street remain vivid, of local heroes like Charlie Taylor, Basil Watts, Vic Yorke, Stan Flannery and full-back Willie Hargreaves in the amber and black.

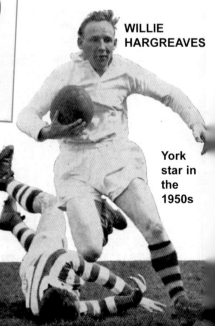

WILLIE HARGREAVES

York star in the 1950s

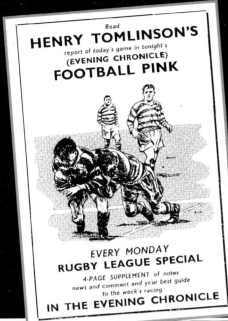

Read
HENRY TOMLINSON'S
report of today's game in tonight's
(EVENING CHRONICLE)
FOOTBALL PINK

EVERY MONDAY
RUGBY LEAGUE SPECIAL
4-PAGE SUPPLEMENT of notes
news and comment and your best guide
to the week's racing
IN THE EVENING CHRONICLE

The next few pages present a quick walk down memory lane for those who remember being a Rugby League supporter in years gone by in the days when when many things were different. Matches were played on Saturday afternoons and for a lot of people Saturday morning would have been spent at work. There was no local radio to provide commentary, instead it was the printed word which provided the up to the minute information for Rugby League fans who, within an hour of the final whistle being blown, could be reading a blow by blow report of their game in a multitude of newspaper "football specials" - the greens, the pinks or the buffs - as illustrated (left) by one of best known reporters Henry Tomlinson writing in the Manchester *"Evening Chronicle"* Football Pink.

It's easy to see that those were the days when men would work Saturday mornings then go straight to the match in the afternoon. This is Whitehaven's Recreation Ground in the mid '50s and a fine assortment of spectators, including bus-conductors and postmen, enjoy a diving try at the corner by Whitehaven winger Bill Smith against Warrington.

Lions tours every four years and Great Britain playing Tests against Australia at the Sydney Cricket Ground - plus Workington Town players in the British team.
(Above) action from the 1962 tour as Great Britain second-rower Brian Edgar shapes to pass to prop Norman Herbert. Edgar is wearing number six, his tour jersey number on the 1962 Lions tour.

(Right) British fans at home could read all the news from the tour by the one and only Eddie Waring, first in the old *"Sunday Pictorial,"* and later the *"Sunday Mirror."*
Eddie first accompanied a Lions touring team when he travelled with the "Indomitables" in 1946, and it was his proud record of being the only man to cover every post-war tour right up to 1970. Eddie would also put on film shows so fans could see for themselves the action from the Tests in Australia.

The one and only Eddie Waring writes each week in the

Sunday Mirror

The paper that cares about Rugby League

Never was there a more unlikely look-ing Rugby League player than Brian Bevan (above) but he was the greatest try-scorer in the history of the game. When Warrington came to town every-body went just to see Bevan in action.

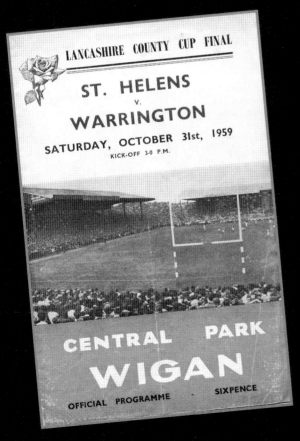

Oldham and Swinton - giants of the game in :ancashire and recognised as two of the most entertaining football sides around. Yet both were fated never to play at Wembley. (Above) Oldham half-back Brian Fallon is tackled by Swinton's Bobby Fleet in a match at the Watersheddings

(Left) Lancashire Cup Finals, highlights of the Autumn and usually played at either Central Park or Station Road. The first of the famous "All Four Cups" up for grabs every season.

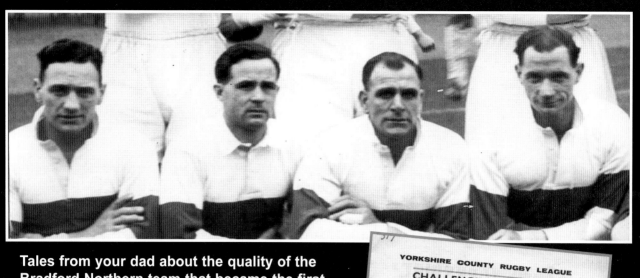

Tales from your dad about the quality of the Bradford Northern team that became the first side to go to three consecutive Wembley Cup Finals. (Above) Donald Ward, W.T.H. Davies, Eric Batten and the captain Ernest Ward.

(Right) Yorkshire Cup Finals with programmes printed by Gideon Shaw of Castleford. As well as being a printer Mr. Shaw was also the manager of the Great Britain team which won the first World Cup in France in 1954.

(Below) When Hull K.R. came north and signed both Bill Holliday and Frank Foster. This Robins team were Yorkshire Cup winners in 1966, beating Featherstone Rovers in the Final. They are, left to right, (Standing): Brian Tyson, Joby Shaw, Bill Holliday, Frank Fox, Mike Blackmore, Terry Major, John Moore. (In front): Arthur Bunting, Roger Millward, Frank Foster (Capt.), Chris Young, Cyril Kellett, David Elliott. (Insets): Peter Flanagan and Alan Burwell.

YORKSHIRE COUNTY RUGBY LEAGUE

CHALLENGE CUP FINAL
1962

HULL K.R. v HUNSLET

SATURDAY, OCTOBER 27th
At HEADINGLEY, LEEDS · Kick-off 3.0 p.m.

Official Souvenir Programme · Price 6d.

Gideon Shaw, Printer, Castleford.

Torn out newspaper cuttings with a picture of Phil Jackson, one of the most stylish centres to play the game. He went with Barrow to three Wembleys in the 'fifties and was one of the young heroes of the first World Cup triumph in 1954.

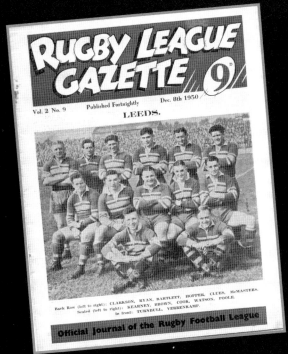

"Rugby League Gazette," an excellent magazine which got the support of the RFL in its circulation wars with Stanley Chadwick's *"Review"* when R.L. fans had plenty of choice.

Looks like Tony's in trouble here - David Hill restrains his front-row colleague Tony Fisher as the touch-judge raises his flag during a Bradford v. Featherstone match at Odsal.

Don't miss your
"RUGBY LEAGUE JOURNAL"

(The Original Spirit of 'Open Rugby')

Published quarterly the *"Rugby League Journal"* brings you four issues per year of high quality literature. If you enjoy the nostalgia of looking back on the game you used to know, its players, teams and famous events, with every issue illustrated with a wonderful collection of old black and white photographs all printed on glossy art paper, the *"Rugby League Journal"* is for you. Mixed with in-depth analysis and comment on current affairs in the world of Rugby League from writers with vast experience in the game, plus book reviews and obituaries, every issue of the *"Rugby League Journal"* provides a hugely enjoyable mix of history, memorabilia and comment.

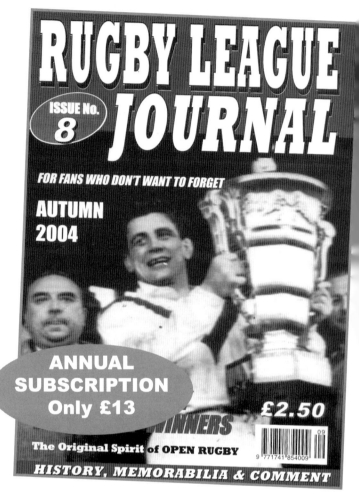

ENSURE YOU DON'T MISS AN ISSUE BY TAKING A SUBSCRIPTION

To book your annual subscription and receive four consecutive issues of the "Journal" just send a cheque or postal order for £13-00 (made payable to *"Rugby League Journal"*), not forgetting to tell us your name and full postal address. Send to:
Rugby League Journal, P.O.Box 22, Egremont, Cumbria, CA23 3WA.
E-mail: rugbyleague.journal@virgin.net   Sales enquiries: Telephone: 01946 814249
(All new suscriptions will be started with the latest issue which is issue number 8 - illustrated above; unless you request to start with another issue.
Individual sample copies available price £3.50 each (including postage & packing)
Overseas subscription rates on request.

For more news of "Rugby League Journal" - see our web-site at
www.rugbyleaguejournal.com

GREAT SCOTS

(Above) The most capped Scotsman of them all, George Fairbairn, in action for Great Britain against Australia during the 1979 Lions tour. Steve Rogers is the Australian player attempting to tackle George.

As the inspirational leader of Great Britain's winning team in the inaugral World Cup 50 years ago, Dave Valentine is, without doubt, Rugby League's most famous Scotsman. A native of Hawick he was one of several excellent rugby footballers to leave the Borders and head for Huddersfield, most notable among them Valentine's coach at Fartown Alex Fiddes. Considering so few Scots have gone on to be capped by Great Britain at full international level, it was remarkable that a second man from the Borders also played a very important role in that famous World Cup win back in 1954 - winger David Rose. A former Rugby Union international, he won four Great Britain caps, all of them in the 1954 World Cup, scoring two crucial tries in the Final win over France at the Parc des Princes.

The Scot who played more times for Great Britain than any other

Dave Valentine in action for Britain on the 1954 Lions tour.

remains full-back George Fairbairn, with 17 caps. Fairbairn came down from Kelso to sign for Wigan in 1974 and within six months of making his Rugby League debut he won international honours (for England!) in the 1975 World Championships. He first played for the full Great Britain team in the 1977 World Series and went on to captain Great Britain in Test football. Another full-back from Kelso (via Workington) Alan Tait appeared in 10 internationals for Great Britain - plus another four as substitute.

The full list of Scottish Great Britain players with the number of caps they won is: **George Fairbairn 17 ; Dave Valentine 15; Alan Tait 10 (plus 4 subs.); Charlie Renilson 7 (plus 1 sub.); David Rose 4; George "Happy" Wilson 3; Roy Kinnear 1; Drew Turnbull 1 and Rob Valentine 1.**

In addition players with Scottish birth credentials who played for Great Britain are Hugh Waddell (5) and Billy McGinty (4).

2004 The year in Australia

Canterbury-Bankstown came through a play-off series of the highest quality football to win the NRL Premiership in Australia for 2004. The Bulldogs beat the Sydney Roosters 16-13 in the Grand Final with a display of tenacity, power and determination that made them deserved winners over a Roosters side that could not give legend Brad Fittler the fairytale send off he might have dreamt of as he played his last game before retirement.

None was better for Canterbury than mighty Willie Mason in the pack, whose Grand Final display won him the Clive Churchill Medal as the man-of-the-match. Mason came of age in the 2004 season, backing up his exploits on the 2003 Kangaroo tour with a new maturity. It was the eighth Premiership in Canterbury's history, and their first since 1995. For many, it was the Grand Final that should have been played two years earlier when the Bulldogs led the competition only to be penalised out of it because of their abuse of the salary cap - and the club put a series of very unpleasant off-field problems in the pre-season behind them to win through, with Kiwis Matt Utai and teenager Sonny Bill Williams to the fore.

Canterbury's long serving captain Steve Price said farewell to the Bulldogs at the end of 2004 and will be heading for Auckland in 2005. Unfortunately, injury prevented him from playing in Canterbury's Grand Final victory in october. Here, Price feels the might of the North Queensland Cowboys defence.

Fittler's farewell season had earlier had the perfect script when he responded to the call of his mentor Phil Gould and returned to representative football in the State of Origin series. New South Wales were one up in the series after a dour first-up victory over Queensland won by a "golden point" drop goal by Shaun Timmins in extra-time in Sydney, when coach Gould sent the call to Fittler to don the sky blue number six jersey again. Brad said "yes" and immediately set up a head-to-head contest of rare vintage with Queensland skipper Darren Lockyer in Brisbane. But, in front of a Suncorp (formerly Lang Park) Stadium record crowd of 52,478, Lockyer and his Maroons squared the series with a 22-18 win. It was a match of breathtaking quality with Queensland's victory sealed by a wonder-try by young Billy Slater.

The third and deciding match saw Fittler step out in front of his home crowd in Sydney and inspire NSW to a clinching 36-14 win, he even scored the final Blues try, charging down a kick and waving to the crowd as he strode behind the posts.

A capacity attendance of 82,487 in the Olympic Stadium (now called the Telstra Stadium) put the seal on the most watched Origin series in history - record crowds and record television viewing figures once again showed it to be the highlight of the Rugby League year in Australia. Victory also meant NSW went ahead for the first time ever on the all-time Origin series ledger, 11-10, with two drawn series, and allowed their controversial coach Phil Gould to step down (for good this time, he says) as the most successful coach in State of Origin history.

Gould finished with a record six series wins, one drawn and one lost; and his 14 matches won was three more than both Wayne Bennett and Arthur Beetson managed for Queensland in their distinguished coaching careers. Gould called a halt after spanning 12 years as part of State of Origin, and the controversy that followed him had become the media focal point of the annual event just as much as Queenslanders Wally Lewis or Gorden Tallis had been in the past.

Phil Gould remained one of the highest profile media analysts in Australian Rugby League in 2004 and was unbending in his views that the NRL was making a massive mistake in their decision not to admit a 16th team for 2005. The bids from both the Gold Coast and Central Coast (Gosford) were extremely strong, yet both were rejected by the NRL Board.

Gould said what everybody knew, that the game was still effectively being controlled by Rupert Murdoch's News Limited - all three Australian Rugby League representatives on the NRL Board voted "yes" to a 16th team, but all three News Limited representatives said "no." The folly of Rugby League turning its back on areas like the Gold Coast and Central Coast (alienating one of the game's most benevolent and influential supporters in John Singleton in the process) was immediately confimed when the Rugby Union wasted no time in allocating a fourth "Super 12" team to be set up in Australia.

Pressure from the cash rich Rugby Union to snap up more talent from Rugby League was never far away in 2004, and there was a media frenzy before the injured NSW and Australian captain Andrew Johns finally resisted the temptations of the 15-aside code to re-sign for his home town club the Newcastle Knights. The next big target appears to be Canterbury stand-off Braith Anasta, one of the pin-up boys of Sydney Rugby League.

The biggest success story of the 2004 season in Australia was the emergence, at last, of the North Queensland Cowboys as a play-off team after ten years of failure. So many have tried before over the past decade, but it was coach Graham Murray - formerly of Leeds and the Sydney Roosters - who finally created a winning outfit and awoke the sleeping giants from sub-tropical Townsville. After finishing in seventh place in the league, North Queensland created a massive shock when they went to Sydney and beat Canterbury 30-22 in the play-offs. They followed up by knocking out their Queensland big brothers, the Brisbane Broncos, 10-nil and then were desperately unlucky to lose 19-16 to the Sydney Roosters in the final eliminator before the Grand Final. At the other end of the table, South Sydney finished with the wooden-spoon again with the desperately disappointing New Zealand Warriors just ahead of them on points difference. But Souths, the club with most Premierships in the history of the game in Australia, surprised everybody by recruiting Shane Richardson as their chief executive mid-season from the reigning premiers Penrith. And when Souths parted company with Paul Langmack as their coach, Richardson wasted little time in appointing Shaun McRae, his former colleague from Hull and Gateshead days, to take over with the Rabbitohs for 2005.

2004 was a great year individually for hooker Danny Buderus, despite Newcastle's failure to make the top-eight play-offs. He captained NSW to their State of Origin series win and later was named as the "Dally M" award winner, effectively making him Australian Rugby League's player-of-the-year.

With international Rugby League now taking such a

Dominating figures in 2004 in Australia, Brad Fittler greeted by his mentor Phil Gould after a final State of Origin game for both in Sydney.

back seat in Australia behind the club competition and the State of Origin, the only chance the Aussie public got to see the green and gold in action in 2004 was the Anzac Test against New Zealand in April, played at Newcastle. A crowd of 21,537 at the redeveloped "Energy Australia Stadium" saw captain Darren Lockyer inspire the Aussies to a 37-10 win over a weakened Kiwi side who had exceeded expectations by holding Australia to 11-10 at half-time. As well as Lockyer, Australia's stars were the Newcastle Knights wing-centre partnership of Timana Tahu and Matthew Gidley, playing on their home ground.

It was the first Test in the new regime of Wayne Bennett as Australia' coach. He had been appointed following the sacking of Chris Anderson shortly after the return of his 2003 Kangaroo tourists who had achieved a three-nil clean sweep Ashes series over Great Britain. Bizarrely, Anderson was to later find himself coaching a Rugby Union team in Wales.

The rise of the North Queensland Cowboys to be a power alongside Brisbane augers well for Rugby League in the state of Queensland, and there were more positive signs in the 2004 Queensland Cup, the competition below NRL level. After many years of dwindling crowds and playing second fiddle to the mighty Broncos in Brisbane, the Queensland Cup in 2004 saw a return of fans as both active spectators and TV viewers. In a Grand Final full of high drama and fine football at Suncorp Stadium, the Burleigh Bears won the Cup after a 22-18 extra-time victory over Brisbane Easts. The match-winning try came in the 97th minute from Burleigh (no pun intended!) prop Shane O'Flanaghan (formerly with Toulouse in France). In the beaten Easts team were former Test players Darren Smith (ex-St.Helens) and Steve Renouf (ex-Wigan.)

BRITS IN AUSSIE GRAND FINALS

Familiar faces for Castleford fans as Kevin Ward joins Ronnie Gibbs in lifting the Winfield Cup after Manly's victory over Canberra in the 1987 Grand Final. Ward was flown out to Sydney from England especially for this Grand Final and justified Manly's faith in him by playing a starring role in the victory.

Ever since the first Kangaroo touring team came to Britain in 1908, Australian players became much sought after by the leading English clubs. But - despite Britain's domination of the Ashes during the first half of the 20th Century - the movement of players in the opposite direction remained largely unknown until the mid 1960s.

The great Cumbrian second-rower Dick Huddart and former Wigan stand-off David Bolton became the first Englishmen to play in a Sydney Grand Final when they lined up on opposite sides in 1966 - Huddart scoring a try in St.George's win over Bolton's Balmain.

A record four British players appeared in the 1973 Grand Final, with Malcolm Reilly in the victorious Manly side and Tommy Bishop, Bob Wear and Cliff Watson playing for their opponents Cronulla. Reilly also coached a Premiership winning team when his Newcastle Knights won the 1997 Grand Final.

The full roll of honour of British players to achieve the distinction of playing in a Grand Final in Australia's leading competition is:

Dick Huddart (St.George) 1966 winners.
David Bolton (Balmain) 1966 losers; 1969 winners.
Mervyn Hicks (Canterbury) 1967 losers.
Ken Batty (St.George) 1971 losers.
Malcolm Reilly (Manly-Warringah) 1972 winners; 1973 winners.
Tommy Bishop (Cronulla-Sutherland) 1973 losers.
Cliff Watson (Cronulla-Sutherland) 1973 losers.
Bob Wear (Cronulla-Sutherland) 1973 losers.
Brian Lockwood (Canterbury) 1974 losers.
Phil Lowe (Manly-Warringah) 1976 winners.
Steve Norton (Manly-Warringah) 1976 winners.
Gary Stephens (Manly-Warringah) 1976 winners.
Kevin Ward (Manly-Warringah) 1987 winners.
Ellery Hanley (Balmain) 1988 losers.
Andy Currier (Balmain) 1989 losers.
Shaun Edwards (Balmain) 1989 losers - *substitute.*
Lee Jackson (Newcastle) 1997 winners - *substitute.*
Adrian Morley (Sydney Roosters) 2002 winners, 2003 losers, 2004 losers.
In addition, the South African Len Killeen, who began his Rugby League career in England with St.Helens, was a Grand Final winner with Balmain in 1969.

2004 IN AUSTRALIA

EXIT BRAD

2004 was the year of the modern-day "greats" of Rugby League, Brad Fittler, brought the curtain down on a wonderful career. Fittler enjoyed a fairytale farewell when he agreed to return to the New South Wales side and inspired the Blues to victory in the State of Origin series decider on home soil in Sydney.

The man who has taken over the mantle as the world's greatest player from Fittler and Andrew Johns is Darren Lockyer who captained Australia to victory over the Kiwis in the 2004 Anzac Test (pictured left) in which he had strong support from experienced prop Shane Webcke.

2004 IN FRANCE

FINALE DE LA COUPE
DE FRANCE LORD DERBY
RUGBY À XIII

SAMEDI 15 MAI
19H30
stade albert domec

ORGANISATION

The teams line up before kick off at Carcassonne in the 2004 Lord Derby Cup Final.

(Right) CLAUDE SIRVENT the veteran three-quarter who led St.Gaudens to the French Championship title in 2004.

BRETT TRUDGETT Carcassonne scrum-half.

(Right) ADEL FELLOUS the UTC prop in the Catalans' Cup Final win against Carcassonne.

2004 The year in France

In a year which marked the 70th anniversary of the birth of French Rugby League - a famous landmark which was allowed to slip by almost totally unnoticed - the game in France saw major decisions made in 2004 on which it appears to be gambling its future.

Firstly, confirmation was given that the Perpignan club Union Treiziste Catalane would be accepted into the English Super League from the 2006 season; *secondly*, there was a big surprise when latecomer Nicolas Larrat was elected to lead the French Federation as its new President taking over when Jean-Paul Ferre stepped down; *thirdly*, the new President's regime decided to move the French domestic season yet further into the no-mans-land of summer rugby - presumably just to stay in step with the British.

The 2003-2004 season had already found that playing Rugby League in the south of France throughout June and into July was folly as the top eight clubs saw their already modest crowds crumble even further in the summer heat as they went through a prolonged series of largely meaningless play-off matches to extend the season through to its July 10th Championship Final. Yet, despite that, the new-look French Federation announced that its next season will not kick off until December and will continue until the Championship Final in the first week of August 2005.

By then it should know more about how Perpignan are shaping up for their move into the Super League the following year and what kind of appetite French players, club organisers and their public might have for the game in the heat and the holiday season. Under their current guise of UTC, the Perpignan club did not find things as easy in 2004 as their English coach Steve Deakin might have hoped as they came a cropper to St.Gaudens in the Championship Final played in front of Perpignan's own public.

St.Gaudens beat hot favourites UTC 14-10 to take the Max Rousie Shield and the title of Champions of France for the fourth time in their history since they became a senior club in 1958. Inspired by their two experienced centres Claude Sirvent and Arnaud Dulac alongside a strong Australian contingent including man-of-the-match second-rower Kevin Cook and long serving St.Gaudens men Anthony Golder and Russell Bussian, the "Bears" held out in a last quarter of almost

(Left) Maxime Greseque - half-back who starred in England for Featherstone after Pia's season finished in France.

(Above) Brad Davis playing for Villeneuve, who never recovered from having their four best players spirited away to UTC in Perpignan.

unbearable tension in the Championship Final. UTC had been hoping to complete a double after being successful in winning the Lord Derby Cup, beating Carcassonne 39-24 in a marvellous Final played on May 15th. A noisy and colourful crowd of around 10,000 packed the Stade Albert Domec in Carcassonne - most of them cheering the home town team - in a game that was full of invention, excitement and sportsmanship that was a real credit to the French game. Most of the old fashioned French flair came from Carcassonne who led 24-14 at half-time, before the superior strength and fitness of their full-time opponents enabled them to grind them down with 25 unanswered points in the second-half.

UTC owed much to man-of-the-match in the Cup Final Laurent Frayssinous who took control after his half-back partner Julien Rinaldi had been forced off the field with a shoulder injury. Frayssinous was later to be chosen as the French Rugby League's player-of-the-year for 2004. He was one of four leading international players - the others being Rinaldi and forwards Djamel Fakir and Romain Gagliazzo - who had been prized away from Villeneuve with the offer of full-time contracts as UTC built towards Super League. Whilst that boosted coach Steve Deakin's prospects of having a successful team, it decimated Villeneuve (later player-coached by Australian Brad Davis) who failed to recoup any transfer fees for the loss of their four star players and found themselves so beset by financial problems that they eventually went into administration.

The thought of losing its pioneer club - in the wake of the loss in recent years of St.Esteve (as a stand alone club) Avignon and Tonneins - would be hugely damaging to the French game, and fingers are crossed that a new Villeneuve-sur-Lot club will be formed to ensure the game continues in its spiritual heartland town. Another famous club who underwent the same process a few years ago, Carcassonne, enjoyed a strong resurgence in 2004 - led by a very capable President in Francis Camel and with the vastly experienced Jean Cabrol as manager, the "Canaries" managed to mobilise their public in their thousands for the Cup Final and with recruitment underway for 2005 to go alongside home-town hero Fred Banquet, despite losing young international centre Teddy Sadaoui to UTC, Carcassonne - along with St.Gaudens and Toulouse Olympique - should ensure the full-timers of UTC do not have things all their own way in the French league.

Financial pressures have also forced another merger with Villefranche, one of the just ten clubs left in the elite division, joining forces with Cahors from the lower division.

In the absence of any kind of European Cup tournament the French clubs continued to look to the English Challenge Cup for their cross-channel encounters and UTC (at Hull K.R.), Limoux (at Gateshead) and Pia (at Barrow) all won away on English soil. Limoux - in the Challenge Cup for the first time - then got the dream home draws, beating Halifax before entertaining Wigan. Limoux were hammered but it was a great event for their club and their town. Pia and UTC eventually went down with some

honour away to Super League clubs Huddersfield and Castleford respectively. Sadly, Villeneuve - the club who pioneered the way for French clubs in the Challenge Cup - still couldn't get a home draw and their weakened side succumbed away to York.

On the international front in the Victory Cup in Russia in May, Claude Sirvent captained a shadow French side lacking all its UTC and Carcassonne men who were playing in the Lord Derby Cup Final the same weekend, and they failed to retain the trophy after losing 23-16 to the BARLA Great Britain team - it was the second time within 12 months the French had lost to the British amateurs.

In advance of the 2004 Autumn internationals, the new French president - under the influence of Tas Baitieri - had brought in an Australian coaching "consultant" Mick Aldous to oversee the preparaton of their national teams and look at player development structures. For Nicolas Larrat and his team the aim has to be strengthening the French Elite division with once mighty clubs like Albi, Marseille or Avignon being able to come back into the fold, and building a higher media profile for the game. For Jean-Paul Ferre, who stepped down after becoming the longest serving President in the French Rugby League's history, the time to reflect on 11 years hard work.

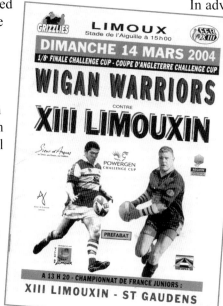

Russians confirmed as an emerging force

Fourteen years after Rugby League was first played in their country, the Russians gave final confirmation in 2004 that they are an emerging force in the game as a nation where it is genuinely played by native Russians who have grown up as Rugby League players and are now able to compete ably with opponents from the established nations - not at top professional level, but nevertheless at a credible standard.

The crowning glory for Russia came in May as they hosted the Victory Cup in Moscow for the second year, and won it. The Russians beat the BARLA Great Britain team by the convincing scoreline of 26-4 in the Final, attended by a reported 15,000 crowd in the Luzhniki Arena. That they were able to beat a team of experienced players like the BARLA team - who had earlier themselves defeated France - speaks volumes for the standard of the Russian side. On their way to the Victory Cup Final Russia had earlier thrashed the USA 64-8 and a team masquerading as "Ireland" but actually

made up largely of players from English Amateur clubs, 64-6.

The Russians were coached by Kiwi Bob Bailey who in April had guided them through a four match tour of the South Island of New Zealand where, once again ,the Russians showed they could compete against experienced League opposition. The Russian tourists won two of their games, 40-32 over the West Coast and 40-10 over Otago, but lost the other two to Canterbury 36-28 and a Tasman selection (a combination of the Nelson and Marlborough regions) 32-16.

The Russians have also got the go-ahead to stage a World Youth Cup (for players aged under-16) in Moscow as their future in Rugby League now looks assured. One less positive note for the Russians in 2004 was the loss of their captain, the big second-rower Kiril Koulemine, who led them on tour to New Zealand and to the Victory Cup, but has since decided to switch to Rugby Union with the French club Agen.

2004 The year in New Zealand

League in New Zealand did not enjoy a vintage year in 2004, and that was long before it had to start grappling with the non-availability of so many leading players as it put a Kiwi side together for the Tri-Nations.

With inspirational former Test captains like Stacey Jones and Stephen Kearney announcing their retirement from international football, as well as hooker Richard Swain who will be joined by Kearney at Hull in 2005, the New Zealand national team had lost its three key creative footballers - the ones who, over recent years, had been the individuals capable of providing that something "extra" in attack and who could win Tests for the Kiwis.

Not that New Zealand has any shortage of players to pick from - its problem is finding pivotal players in key positions to take over from such as Jones and Swain whose absence was crucial when the Kiwis lost 37-10 to Australia in the 2004 Anzac Test, played on 27 April at Newcastle.

New Zealand Rugby League in 2004 was in a quandary. The price paid for putting all your eggs in one basket of creating a sole professional club to play in an overseas competition can be a very heavy one - and while the game in N.Z. glowed with positivity two years ago when the New Zealand (formerly Auckland) Warriors went to the Grand Final, its morale was shattered in 2004 as the Warriors played ineptly at times, suffered heavy defeats and sunk to next to bottom of the table. One-time star players were released from their contracts and allowed to join English clubs, and mid-way through the year they parted company with coach Daniel Anderson - who just two years earlier was seen as a Messiah who had rescued the Warriors and thereby the game's credibility in New Zealand.

Anderson continued in his role as coach to the Kiwi national team, whilst former Doncaster, Castleford and Leeds player Tony Kemp stepped up to the head coach role with the Warriors. Things can only get better for them in 2005, but their problems only served to emphasise the plight of the rest of the domestic game in their country. New Zealand still produces hordes of good young players, the problem is it just cannot provide any opportunity for them to go on and play the game at some kind of professional level in their own country -

STACEY JONES - big Kiwi loss.

outside the chosen few recruited by the Warriors.

The leading domestic competition, the Bartercard Cup, brings together 12 teams from around the country, but its effectiveness is now under severe scrutiny from high profile critics like Graham Lowe. The former Wigan and Kiwi coach, Lowe questioned the validity of the Bartercard Cup when none of its players were deemed suitable for Kiwi selection, despite their need to find new players. Lowe bemoaned the loss of the really strong Auckland club competition of years gone by, and the fiercely fought inter-provincial matches between such as Canterbury, Wellington and the Aucklanders.

For the record, a crowd of only 2,000 was reported for the 2004 Bartercard Cup Grand Final at the Ericsson Stadium in Auckland, in which Mount Albert Lions beat Marist Richmond Brothers 40-20. In years gone by Auckland Grand Finals would attract packed houses to the old Carlaw Park headquarters.

New Zealand Rugby League is the victim of a huge talent drain as promising teenage players head off to Australia, the lucky ones on scholarships with the Aussie clubs, in search of a professional career in the game. The ranks of NRL clubs are now littered with Pacific Islander names who would all have Kiwi qualification should they seek it. Manly have even set up their own Academy in Auckland. Remarkably, there were no less than nine New Zealanders in the Australian Schoolboys team which drew their 2003 series with the Junior Kiwis - among them the hot teenage prospects Benji Marshall and Karmichael Hunt (now the Brisbane Broncos first-grade full-back who declined selection for the senior Kiwi team in 2004 to pursue State of Origin honours with Queensland.) The hottest prospect of all, Sonny-Bill Williams, had no such qualms and made his Test debut for the Kiwis in 2004 as an 18-year-old and looks set to become one of New Zealand's greatest Rugby League players. One of Graham Lowe's suggestions to "re-energise" the game in New Zealand is the creation of an "Origin" contest between the Kiwis and a Pacific Islander team. Remarkably, when the Kiwis played Australia in 2004, for the first time ever not a single one of their 17 players was a Pakeha..

New young talent a healthy sign

says Brisbane Broncos and Australia coach WAYNE BENNETT

It was a year of great achievement for the England Academy Under-18 team in 2004 who, after drawing their series one-all against the Junior Kiwis in New Zealand, went on to gain a first ever win over the Australian Schoolboys on Aussie soil. Earlier the Australians had recorded big wins over both the BARLA Under-18s and the French Schoolboys. This followed the Academy's series win over the Aussie boys in England the previous year. It was a measure of the huge progress made in the English Rugby League's player development programmes allied to the full-time preparation for teenage players with Super League clubs.

The quality of young players and the quality of the environment in which they are developing augers well for Rugby League's future. Here we are pleased to present the comments of Wayne Bennett, one of the most respected figures in the world of Rugby League, on how the game in Australia is shaping up in the area of developing young players - in the firm belief that the very same principles apply to the game in Great Britain. This is what Wayne had to say:

"The emergence of young talent in Rugby League goes in cycles but I truly can't remember a more impressive group of youngsters making a greater impact on the game than the Class of 2004. Billy Slater, Willie Tonga, Karmichael Hunt, Luke Lewis, Brett Anderson ... the list of players in their teens who have stamped their name on the NRL this year just keeps growing.

A young Mal Meninga playing for Brisbane Souths.

"As I marvel at their talents and how well prepared they are for first-grade football my mind wanders back 28 years to the first time I laid eyes on Mal Meninga who was the most advanced, in football terms, 16 or 17-year-old I had seen. The youngsters coming through these days are as amazingly mature, in a football sense, for their age. They're not necessarily mature as people - and I have no doubt 14 and 15-year-olds of my generation were more "street smart" than today's version - but that's another story.

"From a Rugby League viewpoint, it underlines to me how much better the game has got at identifying and nurturing young talent since the days when the one-in-a-million Meninga burst on to the scene. There are a number of reasons the game has become so good at finding new talent, but they can be broken into three:

Saturation television coverage: Boys see the star players all the time and can model themselves on them.

Career path: From a young age, boys can see that football can provide a career. That wasn't an option 30 years ago.

The junior structure: This is the important reason, the whole basis of talent development in Rugby League boasts a tremendous junior structure, thanks to the efforts of the Australian Rugby League - through the ARL Foundation - the Queensland RL and the New South Wales RL, the schools system and the dedication of thousands of volunteer coaches and officials throughout Queensland and New South Wales.

"So, the emergence of so many talented youngsters in the NRL this year has not happened by accident. It's been the result of carefully planned and well-managed grassroots structure. This year has been the first time I've coached a side (at the Broncos) with four players aged under 19 - Karmichael Hunt and Tom Learoyd came through last year's Australian Schoolboys side, while Neville Costigan and Sam Thaiday were Junior Kangaroos. Even before they reached those junior representative teams they had had the benefit of a system which is remarkably healthy despite the challenges being mounted by other codes.

"As long as we keep our eye on the ball and don't slacken our efforts at the grassroots level, we will be able to keep developing the Hunts, the Slaters and the Tongas. And it won't matter what the other codes are doing."

THE England Academy tour squad in 2004 was: Matthew Cook, Brett Ferres, Karl Pryce (all Bradford); **Craig Huby** (Castleford); **Simon Grix** (Halifax); **Carl Ablett, John Gallagher, Ashley Gibson, Jason Golden, Scott Murrell, Lee Smith, Luke Stenchion, Danny Williams** (all Leeds); **Andy Bracek, James Graham** (St.Helens); **Steven Pickersgill** (Warrington); **David Allen, Chris Ashton, James Coyle, Harrison Hansen, Paul Prescott, Joel Tomkins, Desi Williams** (all Wigan).

Amateur Rugby League in 2004

What had been an outstanding season for the traditional amateur game under the auspices of BARLA, suddenly turned into a nightmare at the end as their open-age tour to Australia in July collapsed into disarray. Reports of misbehaviour by some individuals and players coming home, added to an horrendous injury list, saw the tourists unable to fulfil their final fixture. That prompted a full investigation by the Rugby Football League and some very unpleasant media coverage.

It was all such a shame for the Great Britain Amateurs who, for over 25 years, have played such a postive role in sending touring teams to many parts of the world to aid Rugby League development in new countries, and for the current crop of international players who had earlier created history of the right kind by scoring two victories over the full French national team in the space of nine months.

Captained again by **Leigh Miners** loose-forward Tommy Goulden, the Great Britain Amateurs repeated their 12-6 win over France at Whitehaven in 2003 by beating the French again 23-16 in the Victory Cup in Moscow. It was a weakened French team, but still a feather in the BARLA boys' cap to beat them and progress to the Victory Cup Final where they lost to the hosts Russia 26-4. Earlier in the tournament the BARLA team had also beaten the New Zealand Defence side 26-12.

Over a month after the end of the domestic season, the Great Britain Amateur team headed to Australia on that ill-fated tour, and in the sole "Test" match played they lost heavily, 50-24, to the Australian Aboriginals, thus handing back the Perpetual Trophy for the first time since 1998.

Domestically 2003-04 had been a fine season for the BARLA competitions. The ever increasing standards of the leading clubs was illustrated by yet more success over professional sides in the Challenge Cup-with victories for **Sharslton** over Dewsbury, **East Hull** over Swinton and **Dudley Hill** over Keighley.

Siddal were crowned the top team in the National Conference for the second successive season after they beat **West Hull** 18-16 in a thrilling Grand Final at Batley's Mount Pleasant in May. Siddal's inspirations were two well known ex-professionals who hung up their boots after this year's Grand Final triumph, player-coach Mick Shaw and Johnny Lawless.

Perhaps the best news for the amateur game has been the way the BARLA National Cup has recovered much of its appeal since Blackpool was re-established as the venue for the Final at the end of May. Staged now at Bloomfield Road, a ground which once thrilled

Wath Brow called it the "Holy Grail" of Amateur Rugby League and here the Hornets forward Paul Davidson celebrates winning the BARLA National Cup at Blackpool in May. Davidson himself has made an outstanding contribution to the Amateur game, not only at club level with Wath Brow but as a Great Britain international - he played a key role in both BARLA's wins over France in the 2003-04 season and was one of five Wath Brow men who played in the Victory Cup in Russia. Three later signed in the professional ranks for Whitehaven.

to the deeds of footballing legends like Stanley Matthews and Stan Mortensen, **Oldham St.Anne's** won the National Cup in an emotional Final in 2003 and the Saints were back to defend the Cup in 2004 against the Cumbrians from **Wath Brow Hornets.** In a magnificent Final, which seemed to be heading for extra-time, Wath Brow clinched the Cup with a try in the last play of the game by second-rower Mark Troughton. Carl Rudd converted and the final whistle went with the Hornets ahead 25-19. Winning what they described as still the "Holy Grail" of Amateur Rugby League put the seal on a wonderful season for Wath Brow who were crowned Champions of the National Conference Division One (a year after winning Division Two in their first season in the Conference). **East Hull** were Conference Division Two Champions.

New Horizons in 2004

As a player participation sport Rugby League continued to expand its new horizons significantly in 2004. The National League Division Three, an ostensibly summertime amateur competition run under the auspices of the RFL, began its second season expanded to 14 teams with a geographical spread that stretched from Carlisle and Gateshead in the far north to Essex and South London in the south east.

As with the Summer Conference from which National League Three evolved, more time and much work is still required to ensure the content matches the presentation, but the steady progress of clubs in Coventry, Hemel Hempstead and St.Albans gave genuine cause for optimism that Rugby League is building strong foundations outside the north of England. Like the London Skolars in National League Two, they owed much to the presence of colonials, but a glance at the team-sheets of many Super League clubs would show that is no different to some teams in the game's supposed heartlands which have been given millions of pounds over the past few years to develop the game.

Standards varied enormously, with bottom club Essex Eels copping some fearful hidings. Manchester Knights could not fulfil their fixtures at the latter end of the summer season and Carlisle had their problems along the way. Alongside Coventry, Hemel and St.Albans, the strength of the division came from long established amateur clubs - Woolston of Warrington, Dudley Hill of Bradford and Sheffield Hillsborough.

And the best story of the year was the return of the name Bramley to competitive Rugby League - playing under the moniker of the "Buffaloes" and using the fine facilities of ambitious BARLA club Stanningley, the new Bramley drew some excellent crowds to watch them - creating a nice mix between memories of the old days at the Barley Mow and the new face of summer rugby at this level in the year 2004.

The Summer Conference itself expanded to yet more teams, and from what has been a marvellous vehicle for enabling people to play the game in areas where it has not been available before, this year it included some from the traditional northern heartlands of the game - with very mixed results. One of those teams, Widnes Saints, came through to win the Conference title, beating West London Sharks in the final played at St.Albans. But with the game played this summer in some or shape or form in Wales, Scotland and Ireland as well as all parts of England, those horizons continue to expand.

The Varsity Match, contested for the 24th year in 2004, got a wonderful boost by being televised live by BSkyB for the first time. Viewers enjoyed a hugely entertaining match as Oxford beat Cambridge 29-16.

And a very significant anniverary occurred in 2004 as Rugby League in the Army celebrated its 10th birthday. After being denied existence for almost 100 years by bigotry, Army Rugby League has come a long way since it was officially formed in April 1994.

Remember the Villagers? Some well known names in this Bramley team pictured at McClaren Field in 1973. Left to right (Standing): Harry O'Keefe (physio), Phil Clegg, Malcolm Craker, Dave Worthy, Michael Thornton, Jack Austin, Dave Sampson, Jones, Graham Idle, Denis Ashman, Keith Holliday (coach). (In front): Arthur Keegan, Barney Ward, Trevor Briggs, Peter Goodchild, John Wolford and Ray Price.

SCHOOLS RUGBY LEAGUE

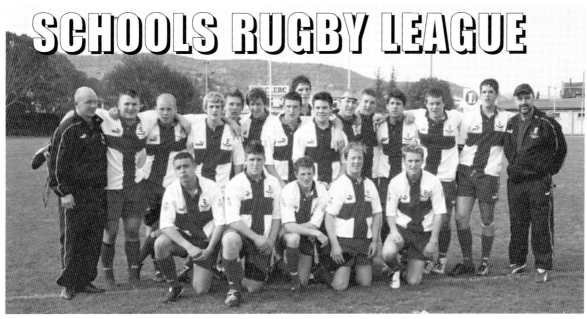

The 2004 English Schools team after winning the first of their two Tests in France during the Easter tour.

Successful year in 2004

Throughout Rugby League's history the game in schools has been an essential part of its foundations. Before the advent of BARLA in 1973 and the dramatic growth in youth Rugby League its clubs managed to provide, playing the game at school was where youngsters took their first steps in Rugby League. Now, it is the Amateur clubs and their army of volunteers who provide all the opportunities to learn the game for children as young as seven or eight years of age - whilst Schools Rugby League is able to provide more high profile stages for them to perform on.

2004 was an excellent year for Schools Rugby League at both elite performance level and in encouraging wider participation. The English Schools team won the *Entente Cordiale* Trophy back from France for the first time since 1999 by winning both Tests on their Easter tour - the first 32-10 at Limoux and the second 40-16 at Pamiers. The English Schools team are the outstanding players aged 16 or under in the country, and whilst all are from BARLA clubs every one of the 22 boys in this year's touring party was also attached to a professional club, as a Scholarship or Junior Academy member.

Signficantly 20 of those were with the Super League clubs St.Helens, Hull, Wigan, Warrington, Leeds, Wakefield and Widnes - and just two from outside Super League, Marc Bainbridge and Daniel Smith who are both with Whitehaven. One of this year's English Schools team, half-back Scott Moore, found himself playing in the Super League for St.Helens later in 2004. *(For a full feature on the 2004 English Schools touring team see the Autumn edition (number eight) of "Rugby League Journal.")*

Meanwhile the Powergen Champion Schools

competition continued to grow at a tremendous rate of knots, with a reported 1,000 teams taking part in the 2003-04 season thus reaching some 16,000 players, both boys and girls. The competition for all the school age groups from years 7 to 11 began at local level, before progressing to regional then national stages, culminating with the finals played in Cardiff on the weekend of the Challenge Cup Final. The youngest age-group, from year 7 (in 2004 being Wade Deacon of Widnes and Whitchurch from Cardiff) got to play in the Millennium Stadium as a curtain-raiser to the Cup Final, maintaining memories of the much loved Under-11s matches that became such a big part of Wembley.

Powergen Champion Schools 2003-04

Year 7
Winners: WADE DEACON (Widnes)
Runners-up: WHITCHURCH (Cardiff)

Year 8
Winners: OUTWOOD GRANGE (Wakefeld)
Runners-up: ST.AUGUSTINE'S (St.Helens)

Year 9
Winners: ST.CUTHBERT'S (St.Helens)
Runners-up: AIREDALE HIGH (Castleford)

Year 10
Winners: ST.JOHN FISHER (Wigan)
Runners-up: WILLIAM BEAMONT (Warrington)

Year 11
Winners: ST.JOHN FISHER (Wigan)
Runners-up: COUNTHILL (Oldham)

GIRLS - Year 7
Winners: QUEENSBURY (Bradford)
Runners-up: CARDINAL NEWMAN (Warrington)

The Championship

Until the arrival of Super League and the changing of the season undermined the position of the Challenge Cup, the Championship always took second place in publicity and prestige in the world of Rugby League - such was the massive appeal of Wembley. But, for the real purists of the game, winning the Championship always was the ultimate accolade as the true measure of a team's ability. Especially so in the days when the Championship Final was played the week after the Wembley Final and became synonymous with huge crowds at Maine Road, Manchester and Odsal Stadium, Bradford. Now the staging of the Super League Grand Final in Manchester before packed houses has brought those great days of the Championship Final back to life. In days gone by the magic of making the "Top Four" was a target for every club in the League, just as the "Top Six" has now become the aim for the teams in the Super League. Even in the eras of Two Divisions in Rugby League with the Champions being decided on the first-past-the-post system, the fascination with end of season play-offs was maintained by the introduction of the Premiership.

When two divisions were introduced to Rugby League in the sixties and contested for two seasons before being abandoned by public demand, Swinton won the Championship both times, in 1962-63 and 1963-64. (Above) we see Swinton's captain Albert Blan receiving the famous old Championship trophy after the first of those wins in 1963. The Lions were the great entertainers of Rugby League at that time.

ALL THE RUGBY LEAGUE CHAMPIONSHIP WINNERS AND RUNNERS-UP

Year	Winners	Runners-up	Year	Winners	Runners-up
1895-96	Manningham	Halifax	1915-19	*No competition during World War One*	
1896-1901	*No competition – County Leagues only*		1919-20	Hull	Huddersfield
1901-02	Broughton Rangers	Salford	1920-21	Hull	Hull K.R.
1902-03	Halifax	Salford	1921-22	Wigan	Oldham
1903-04	Bradford	Salford	1922-23	Hull K.R.	Huddersfield
1904-05	Oldham	Bradford	1923-24	Batley	Wigan
1905-06	Leigh	Hunslet	1924-25	Hull K.R.	Swinton
1906-07	Halifax	Oldham	1925-26	Wigan	Warrington
1907-08	Hunslet	Oldham	1926-27	Swinton	St.Helens Recs.
1908-09	Wigan	Oldham	1927-28	Swinton	Featherstone
1909-10	Oldham	Wigan	1928-29	Huddersfield	Leeds
1910-11	Oldham	Wigan	1929-30	Huddersfield	Leeds
1911-12	Huddersfield	Wigan	1930-31	Swinton	Leeds
1912-13	Huddersfield	Wigan	1931-32	St.Helens	Huddersfield
1913-14	Salford	Huddersfield	1932-33	Salford	Swinton
1914-15	Huddersfield	Leeds	1933-34	Wigan	Salford
			1934-35	Swinton	Warrington

CHAMPIONSHIP WINNERS

Tommy Smales (Huddersfield)
Champions 1961-62

Harold Poynton (Wakefield)
Champions 1967-68

John Burnett (Halifax
Champions 1964-65

1935-36	Hull	Widnes	**1972-73**	Dewsbury	Leeds
1936-37	Salford	Warrington	**1973-74**	Salford	St.Helens
1937-38	Hunslet	Leeds	**1974-75**	St.Helens	Wigan
1938-39	Salford	Castleford	**1975-76**	Salford	Featherstone Rovers
1939-40	Bradford	Swinton	**1976-77**	Featherstone Rovers	St.Helens
1940-41	Bradford	Wigan	**1977-78**	Widnes	Bradford
1941-42	Dewsbury	Bradford	**1978-79**	Hull K.R.	Warrington
1942-43	Dewsbury*	Halifax	**1979-80**	Bradford	Widnes
1943-44	Wigan	Dewsbury	**1980-81**	Bradford	Warrington
1944-45	Bradford	Halifax	**1981-82**	Leigh	Hull
1945-46	Wigan	Huddersfield	**1982-83**	Hull	Hull K.R.
1946-47	Wigan	Dewsbury	**1983-84**	Hull K.R.	Hull
1947-48	Warrington	Bradford	**1984-85**	Hull K.R.	St.Helens
1948-49	Huddersfield	Warrington	**1985-86**	Halifax	Wigan
1949-50	Wigan	Huddersfield	**1986-87**	Wigan	St.Helens
1950-51	Workington Town	Warrington	**1987-88**	Widnes	St.Helens
1951-52	Wigan	Bradford	**1988-89**	Widnes	Wigan
1952-53	St.Helens	Halifax	**1989-90**	Wigan	Leeds
1953-54	Warrington	Halifax	**1990-91**	Wigan	Widnes
1954-55	Warrington	Oldham	**1991-92**	Wigan	St.Helens
1955-56	Hull	Halifax	**1992-93**	Wigan	St.Helens
1956-57	Oldham	Hull	**1993-94**	Wigan	Bradford
1957-58	Hull	Workington Town	**1994-95**	Wigan	Leeds
1958-59	St.Helens	Hunslet	**1995-96**	Wigan	Leeds
1959-60	Wigan	Wakefield Trinity	**1996**	St.Helens	Wigan
1960-61	Leeds	Warrington	**1997**	Bradford	London Broncos
1961-62	Huddersfield	Wakefield Trinity	**1998**	Wigan	Leeds
1962-63	Swinton	St.Helens	**1999**	St.Helens	Bradford
1963-64	Swinton	Wigan	**2000**	St.Helens	Wigan
1964-65	Halifax	St.Helens	**2001**	Bradford	Wigan
1965-66	St.Helens	Halifax	**2002**	St.Helens	Bradford
1966-67	Wakefield Trinity	St.Helens	**2003**	Bradford	Wigan
1967-68	Wakefield Trinity	Hull K.R.	**2004**	Leeds	Bradford
1968-69	Leeds	Castleford			
1969-70	St.Helens	Leeds			
1970-71	St.Helens	Wigan			
1971-72	Leeds	St.Helens			

(* In the war-time season of 1942-43 the Championship was declared void after Dewsbury were found to have played an ineligible player in the Championship Final against Halifax.)

The Challenge Cup

The magic moment in the lives of so many Rugby League players, walking out onto the Wembley turf at the Challenge Cup Final. Here Wigan Chairman Mr. Bill Gore and skipper Eric Ashton lead their team out at Wembley in 1959, alongside them their opponents from Hull with Arthur Keegan at the front on the picture. Immediately behind Eric Ashton are Fred Griffiths and Billy Boston. Wigan beat Hull that day 30-13.

ALL THE RUGBY LEAGUE CHALLENGE CUP WINNERS AND RUNNERS-UP

Year	Winners	Runners-up	Year	Winners	Runners-up
1897	Batley	St.Helens	1927	Oldham	Swinton
1898	Batley	Bradford	1928	Swinton	Warrington
1899	Oldham	Hunslet	1929	Wigan	Dewsbury
1900	Swinton	Salford	1930	Widnes	St.Helens
1901	Batley	Warrington	1931	Halifax	York
1902	Broughton Rangers	Salford	1932	Leeds	Swinton
1903	Halifax	Salford	1933	Huddersfield	Warrington
1904	Halifax	Warrington	1934	Hunslet	Widnes
1905	Warrington	Hull K.R.	1935	Castleford	Huddersfield
1906	Bradford	Salford	1936	Leeds	Warrington
1907	Warrington	Oldham	1937	Widnes	Keighley
1908	Hunslet	Hull	1938	Salford	Barrow
1909	Wakefield Trinity	Hull	1939	Halifax	Salford
1910*	Leeds	Hull	1940	*No competition.*	
1911	Broughton Rangers	Wigan	1941	Leeds	Halifax
1912	Dewsbury	Oldham	1942	Leeds	Halifax
1913	Huddersfield	Warrington	1943	Dewsbury	Leeds
1914	Hull	Wakefield T.	1944	Bradford	Wigan
1915	Huddersfield	St.Helens	1945	Huddersfield	Bradford
1916-1919	*No Competition during War years*		1946	Wakefield Trinity	Wigan
1920	Huddersfield	Wigan	1947	Bradford	Leeds
1921	Leigh	Halifax	1948	Wigan	Bradford
1922	Rochdale Hornets	Hull	1949	Bradford	Halifax
1923	Leeds	Hull	1950	Warrington	Widnes
1924	Wigan	Oldham	1951	Wigan	Barrow
1925	Oldham	Hull K.R.	1952	Workington Town	Featherstone
1926	Swinton	Oldham	1953	Huddersfield	St.Helens
			1954*	Warrington	Halifax

Challenge Cup Final memories - (above) Halifax captain Alvin Ackerley congratulates St.Helens skipper Alan Prescott after Saints had won the Cup for the first time in the 1956 Final. (Right) Wembley nostalgia, programmes from 1975 and 1961.

1955	Barrow	Workington	**1981**	Widnes	Hull K.R.
1956	St.Helens	Halifax	**1982***	Hull	Widnes
1957	Leeds	Barrow	**1983**	Featherstone R.	Hull
1958	Wigan	Workington	**1984**	Widnes	Wigan
1959	Wigan	Hull	**1985**	Wigan	Hull
1960	Wakefield Trinity	Hull	**1986**	Castleford	Hull K.R.
1961	St.Helens	Wigan	**1987**	Halifax	St.Helens
1962	Wakefield Trinity	Huddersfield	**1988**	Wigan	Halifax
1963	Wakefield Trinity	Wigan	**1989**	Wigan	St.Helens
1964	Widnes	Hull K.R.	**1990**	Wigan	Warrington
1965	Wigan	Hunslet	**1991**	Wigan	St.Helens
1966	St.Helens	Wigan	**1992**	Wigan	Castleford
1967	Featherstone R.	Barrow	**1993**	Wigan	Widnes
1968	Leeds	Wakefield T.	**1994**	Wigan	Leeds
1969	Castleford	Salford	**1995**	Wigan	Leeds
1970	Castleford	Wigan	**1996**	St.Helens	Bradford
1971	Leigh	Leeds	**1997**	St.Helens	Bradford
1972	St.Helens	Leeds	**1998**	Sheffield Eagles	Wigan
1973	Featherstone R.	Bradford	**1999**	Leeds	London Broncos
1974	Warrington	Featherstone	**2000**	Bradford	Leeds
1975	Widnes	Warrington	**2001**	St.Helens	Bradford
1976	St.Helens	Widnes	**2002**	Wigan	St.Helens
1977	Leeds	Widnes	**2003**	Bradford	Leeds
1978	Leeds	St.Helens	**2004**	St.Helens	Wigan
1979	Widnes	Wakefield T.			
1980	Hull K.R.	Hull			

*(*Denotes Cup decided after replay of a drawn Final.)*

The Lance Todd Trophy

Man-of-the-match awards have become ten-a-penny in many sports, most especially Rugby League, to the point where they are pretty superfluous. But one which remains a recognised and cherished honour is the one that became one of the first such awards anywhere in the world of sport when it was introduced back in 1946 - the Lance Todd Trophy.

A memorial to Lance Todd (pictured) the award is presented to the man of the match in the Challenge Cup Final, the winner being decided by a ballot of members of the Rugby League Writers' Association. The award was instituted in time for the first post-war Cup Final at Wembley in 1946 following the iniatives of Australian-born pioneer Harry Sunderland, former British Lions tour manager and Warrington official Bob Anderton, and Yorkshire journalist John Bapty. Lance Todd had first come to England from his native New Zealand as a member of the very first Rugby League (Northern Union) international touring team, the "All Golds" of 1907. He subsequently signed for Wigan and stayed in this country, later to become one of the game's most charismatic figures as manager-coach of the famous Salford "Red Devils" in the 1930s. Lance Todd had met an untimely death in a road accident near Oldham during war-time service in 1942.

THE ROLL OF HONOUR - LANCE TODD TROPHY WINNERS

1946 **Billy Stott** Wakefield Trinity (v. Wigan) *Centre*
1947 **Willie Davies** Bradford Northern (v.Leeds) *Stand-off*
1948 **Frank Whitcombe** Bradford Northern* (v. Wigan) *Prop*
1949 **Ernest Ward** Bradford Northern (v. Halifax) *Centre*
1950 **Gerry Helme** Warrington (v. Widnes) *Scrum-half*
1951 **Cec Mountford** Wigan (v. Barrow) *Stand-off*
1952 **Billy Ivison** Workington (v. Featherstone) *Loose-forward*
1953 **Peter Ramsden** Huddersfield (v. St.Helens) *Stand-off*
1954 **Gerry Helme** Warrington (v. Halifax) *Scrum-half*
1955 **Jack Grundy** Barrow (v. Workington Town) *Second-row*
1956 **Alan Prescott** St.Helens (v. Halifax) *Prop*
1957 **Jeff Stevenson** Leeds (v. Barrow) *Scrum-half*
1958 **Rees Thomas** Wigan (v. Workington Town) *Scrum-half*
1959 **Brian McTigue** Wigan (v. Hull) *Second-row*
1960 **Tommy Harris** Hull* (v. Wakefield Trinity) *Hooker*
1961 **Dick Huddart** St.Helens (v. Wigan) *Second-row*
1962 **Neil Fox** Wakefield Trinity (v. Huddersfield) *Centre*
1963 **Harold Poynton** Wakefield Trinity (v. Wigan) *Stand-off*
1964 **Frank Collier** Widnes (v. Hull K.R.) *Prop*
1965 **Ray Ashby** Wigan (v. Hunslet) *Full-back*
       Brian Gabbitas Hunslet* (v. Wigan) *Stand-off*
1966 **Len Killeen** St.Helens (v. Wigan) *Winger*
1967 **Carl Dooler** Featherstone Rovers (v. Barrow) *Scrum-half*
1968 **Don Fox** Wakefield Trinity* (v. Leeds) *Prop*
1969 **Malcolm Reilly** Castleford (v. Salford) *Loose-forward*
1970 **Bill Kirkbride** Castleford (v. Wigan) *Second-row*
1971 **Alex Murphy** Leigh (v. Leeds) *Scrum-half*
1972 **Kel Coslett** St.Helens (v. Leeds) *Loose-forward*
1973 **Steve Nash** Featherstone (v. Bradford) *Scrum-half*
1974 **Derek Whitehead** Warrington (v. Featherstone) *Full-back*
1975 **Ray Dutton** Widnes (v. Warrington) *Full-back*
1976 **Geoff Pimblett** St.Helens (v. Widnes) *Full-back*
1977 **Steve Pitchford** Leeds (v. Widnes) *Prop*
1978 **George Nicholls** St.Helens* (v. Leeds) *Second-row*
1979 **David Topliss** Wakefield Trinity* (v. Widnes) *Stand-off*
1980 **Brian Lockwood** Hull K.R. (v. Hull) *Prop*
1981 **Mick Burke** Widnes (v. Hull K.R.) *Full-back*
1982 **Eddie Cunningham** Widnes (v. Hull) *Centre*
1983 **David Hobbs** Featherstone (v. Hull) *Second-row*
1984 **Joe Lydon** Widnes (v. Wigan) *Centre*
1985 **Brett Kenny** Wigan (v. Hull) *Stand-off*

1986 **Bob Beardmore** Castleford (v. Hull K.R.) *Scrum-half*
1987 **Graham Eadie** Halifax (v. St.Helens) *Full-back*
1988 **Andy Gregory** Wigan (v. Halifax) *Scrum-half*
1989 **Ellery Hanley** Wigan (v. St.Helens) *Loose-forward*
1990 **Andy Gregory** Wigan (v. Warrington) *Scrum-half*
1991 **Denis Betts** Wigan (v. St.Helens) *Second-row*
1992 **Martin Offiah** Wigan (v. Castleford) *Winger*
1993 **Dean Bell** Wigan (v. Widnes) *Loose-forward*
1994 **Martin Offiah** Wigan (v. Leeds) *Winger*
1995 **Jason Robinson** Wigan (v. Leeds) *Winger*
1996 **Robbie Paul** Bradford* (v. St.Helens) *Scrum-half*
1997 **Tommy Martyn** St.Helens (v. Bradford) *Stand-off*
1998 **Mark Aston** Sheffield Eagles (v. Wigan) *Scrum-half*
1999 **Leroy Rivett** Leeds (v. London Broncos) *Winger*
2000 **Henry Paul** Bradford (v. Leeds) *Stand-off*
2001 **Sean Long** St.Helens (v. Bradford) *Scrum-half*
2002 **Kris Radlinski** Wigan (v. St.Helens) *Full-back*
2003 **Gary Connolly** Leeds* (v. Bradford) *Full-back*
2004 **Sean Long** St.Helens (v. Wigan) *Scrum-half*

(* denotes losing team in Challenge Cup Final)

NOTE: There have been two drawn Finals - in 1954 Gerry Helme was awarded the Lance Todd Trophy in the replay at Odsal Stadium, in 1982 Eddie Cunningham was awarded the Trophy in the drawn game at Wembley although his team Widnes eventually lost the replay to Hull at Elland Road.

Ray Ashby of Wigan celebrates sharing the Lance Todd Trophy in 1965 with Hunslet's Brian Gabbitas.

FOR FANS WHO DON'T WANT TO FORGET

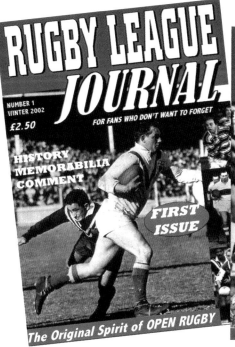

GREAT STORIES

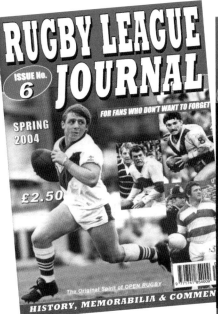

GREAT PICTURES

and GREAT MEMORIES

You can catch up on your reading and some great memories of old style Rugby League with these six back issues of *"Rugby League Journal."* Don't miss these superb collectors' items.

ALL BACK -ISSUES PRICE £3.50 EACH *(incl. p&p)*

All six of the Back Issues illustrated - numbers 1, 4, 5, 6, 7 and 8 are still available. *(Sorry, numbers 2 and 3 are now sold out.)*
To order Back Issues at £3.50 each send cheque/P.O. (payable to "Rugby League Journal") to:
Rugby League Journal, P.O.Box 22, Egremont, Cumbria, CA23 3WA.
E-mail: rugbyleague.journal@virgin.net   www.rugbyleaguejournal.com

GREAT BRITAIN - BEFORE THE INVINCIBLES

Flashback to 1982 and this was a Great Britain selection before playing a trial match against Hull Kingston Rovers at the old Craven Park as part of their preparation before meeting Australia in the Ashes series. Little did anybody know what lay ahead and and that the 1982 Kangaroo "Invincibles" were about to change Rugby League forever. The British players are, left to right, (Standing): Steve Hartley, Kevin Dick, John Joyner, David Watkinson, Steve Norton, Ian Potter, Mike O'Neill, Steve Evans, Peter Smith, Mike Smith, Trevor Skerrett, Ray Tabern, John Basnett, Des Drummond. (Front row): Eric Hughes, Andy Gregory, Paul Prendiville, Les Dyl, George Fairbairn, Steve Nash and David Ward.

The Ultimate Warriors

In a game as physically demanding as Rugby League it takes a tremendous amount of endurance, courage and both physical and mental strength to be able to play the game at first class professional level for a whole decade. To be able to have done it for two decades and more is a quite remarkable achievement, aided of course by the good fortune to have avoided any career threatening injuries along the way. As a tribute to the "Ultimate Warriors" of British sport, on this page we present a list of the top 30 number of appearances in the history of the British game- all first-class club and representative games are included in these records.

**GRAHAM IDLE
- 740 games**

THE TOP 30 PLAYER CAREER APPEARANCE RECORDS

Games	Player and Clubs played for	Career span
928	**Jim Sullivan** (Wigan)	1921-1946
873	**Gus Risman** (Salford, Workington Town, Batley)	1929-1954
828 (28)	**Neil Fox** (Wakefield Trinity, Bradford, Hull K.R., York, Bramley, Huddersfield)	1956-1979
776 (57)	**Jeff Grayshon** (Dewsbury, Bradford, Leeds, Featherstone, Batley)	1969-1995
740 (46)	**Graham Idle** (Bramley, Wakefield, Bradford, Hunslet, Rochdale, Sheffield, Doncaster, Nottingham City, Highfield)	1969-1993
738 (25)	**Colin Dixon** (Halifax, Salford, Hull K.R.)	1961-1981
727 (9)	**Paul Charlton** (Workington Town, Salford, Blackpool Borough)	1961-1981
695 (26)	**Keith Mumby** (Bradford, Sheffield, Keighley, Ryedale-York, Wakefield)	1973-1995
691 (1)	**Ernie Ashcroft** (Wigan, Huddersfield, Warrington)	1942-1962
688	**Brian Bevan** (Warrington, Blackpool Borough)	1945-1964
683 (24)	**John Wolford** (Bramley, Bradford, Dewsbury, Hunslet)	1962-1985
682	**Joe Ferguson** (Oldham)	1899-1923
679	**Joe Oliver** (Huddersfield, Batley, Hull, Hull K.R.)	1923-1945
669 (33)	**John Joyner** (Castleford)	1973-1992
665	**George Carmichael** (Hull K.R., Bradford)	1929-1950
663 (25)	**John Holmes** (Leeds)	1968-1989
662 (28)	**Mal Aspey** (Widnes, Fulham, Wigan, Salford)	1964-1983
651	**Jack Miller** (Warrington, Leigh)	1926-1947
638	**Stanley Brogden** (Bradford, Huddersfield, Leeds, Hull, Rochdale Hornets Salford, Whitehaven)	1927-1948
637	**Ken Gee** (Wigan)	1935-1954
634 (8)	**Ken Gowers** (Swinton)	1954-1973
630	**Eric Batten** (Wakefield Trinity, Hunslet, Bradford, Featherstone Rovers)	1933-1954
629 (11)	**Clive Sullivan** (Hull, Hull K.R., Oldham, Doncaster)	1961-1985
622	**Harry Wilkinson** (Wakefield Trinity)	1930-1949
620 (8)	**Billy Benyon** (St.Helens, Warrington)	1962-1981
618 (13)	**Frank Myler** (Widnes, St.Helens, Rochdale Hornets)	1955-1973
615 (10)	**Geoff Gunney** (Hunslet)	1951-1973
613 (9)	**Terry Clawson** (Featherstone, Bradford, Hull K.R., Leeds, Oldham, York Wakefield Trinity, Huddersfield, Hull)	1957-1980
611 (6)	**John Atkinson** (Leeds, Carlisle)	1966-1983
611 (5)	**Keith Elwell** (Widnes, Barrow)	1969-1986

(Figures in brackets indicate number of appearances as a substitute included in total)

Great Britain Most Capped Players

46	Mick Sullivan
46 (+2)	Garry Schofield
36 (+1)	Ellery Hanley
36 (+4)	Shaun Edwards
33	Martin Offiah
33 (+10)	Daryl Powell
32 (+2)	Denis Betts
31	Billy Boston
31 (+3)	Gary Connolly
30 (+1)	Cliff Watson
30 (+7)	Joe Lydon
29	Andrew Farrell
29	George Nicholls
29	Neil Fox
29 (+1)	Roger Millward
28	Alan Prescott
27	Phil Jackson
27	Alex Murphy
26	Eric Ashton
26	John Atkinson
26 (+1)	Andy Gregory
25	Brian McTigue
25	Jim Sullivan
25	Tommy Harris
25 (+4)	Andy Platt
24	Des Drummond
24	Steve Nash
24	Derek Turner
24 (+1)	Frank Myler
23	David Bolton
23	Andy Goodway
23 (+2)	Chris Hesketh
21 (+1)	Jimmy Thompson
21 (+2)	Paul Sculthorpe
20	Alan Davies
20	Ernest Ward
20	Kris Radlinski
20 (+6)	John Holmes

(Figures in brackets indicate substitute appearances included in the total.)

MICK SULLIVAN

The most capped Great Britain player in Rugby League history - a record jointly held by Garry Schofield. The first of Sullivan's 46 caps came as a Huddersfield player in the 1954 World Cup and the last in the 1963 Ashes series as a York player, and included a record run of 36 consecutive international matches. Mick also played in an additional two matches for Great Britain against France in the years before such games were given full Test status in 1957.

ALEX MURPHY

Won a total of 27 caps for Great Britain, a figure that could have been considerably higher if Alex had not declined to tour with the 1966 Lions and fallen out with the authorities from time to time. Still regarded by many Australians as the best English player they ever saw, Murphy was a teenage prodigy from St.Helens who made his Test debut as an 18-year-old on the 1958 Lions tour and returned to Australia four years later to play a key role in the retention of the Ashes. Alex played his last Test as a Warrington player in the 1971 home series against New Zealand.

(*All figures are up to and including the 2003 Ashes series.)

Lions Tour Captains

1910 - James Lomas (Salford)
1914 - Harold Wagstaff (Huddersfield)
1920 - Harold Wagstaff (Huddersfield)
1924 - Jonty Parkin (Wakefield Trinity)
1928 - Jonty Parkin (Wakefield Trinity)
1932 - Jim Sullivan (Wigan)
1936 - Jim Brough (Leeds)
1946 - Gus Risman (Salford)
1950 - Ernest Ward (Bradford N'thn.)
1954 - Dickie Williams (Hunslet)

1958 - Alan Prescott (St.Helens)
1962 - Eric Ashton (Wigan)
1966 - Harry Poole (Leeds)
1970 - Frank Myler (St.Helens)
1974 - Chris Hesketh (Salford)
1979 - Doug Laughton (Widnes)
1984 - Brian Noble (Bradford Northern)
1988 - Ellery Hanley (Wigan)
1990 - Mike Gregory (Warrington)
(To New Zealand & Papua.N.G. only)

Alan Prescott

1992 - Ellery Hanley (Wigan)
1996 - Andrew Farrell (Wigan)
(To New Zealand, P.N.G. & Fiji only)

GREAT BRITAIN PLAYERS

The complete register of British internationals

(Above) a picture which tells a thousand words about the pride and quality of being a Great Britain Rugby League international as one of the nation's finest sporting captains, Ernest Ward, leads his team out at Headingley in October 1948 alongside the Australians, at the start of another thrilling Ashes series. Behind Ernest is his vice-captain Joe Egan and the other British players in camera are: Jimmy Ledgard, Johnny Lawrenson, Albert Pimblett, Stan McCormick, Willie Horne and Gerry Helme.

Here and on the following pages we present the complete register of players who have appeared for Great Britain in full Test matches and World Cup games from the first one in 1907 to date (i.e. up to and including the 2003 Ashes series as this book was published before any 2004 internationals were played.) Records do not include matches against France before 1957, the year in which Britain-France games were given official Test match status.

KEY: After the player's name we list his total number of Great Britain appearances in brackets with a plus sign indicating substitute appearances, e.g. (5+2); the club(s) he was with, and the years which signify the duration of his G.B. career. The letters **"R.D."** indicate the thirteen men who played in the legendary "Rorke's Drift" Test in 1914.

A

ACKERLEY, Alvin (2) Halifax: 1952-1958.
ADAMS, Les (1) Leeds: 1932.
ADAMS, Mick (11+2) Widnes: 1979-1984.

ANDERSON, Paul (+10) Bradford: 1999 - 2003
ARKWRIGHT, Chris (+2) St.Helens: 1985.
ARKWRIGHT, Jack (6) Warrington: 1936-1937.
ARMITT, Tommy (8) Swinton: 1933-1937.

ASHBY, Ray (2) Liverpool City & Wigan: 1964 - 1965.
ASHCROFT, Ernest (11) Wigan: 1947 - 1954.
ASHCROFT, Kevin (5+1) Leigh & Warrington: 1968 - 1974.
ASHTON, Eric (26) Wigan: 1957 - 1963.
ASHURST, Bill (3) Wigan: 1971 -1972.
ASKIN, Tommy (6) Featherstone Rovers: 1928.
ASPINALL, Willie (1) Warrington: 1966.
ASTON, Len (3) St.Helens: 1947.
ASTON, Mark (+1) Sheffield Eagles: 1991.
ATCHESON, Paul (2+1) St.Helens: 1997.
ATKINSON, Arthur (11) Castleford: 1929 - 1936.
ATKINSON, John (26) Leeds: 1968 - 1980.
AVERY, Bert (4) Oldham: 1910 -1911.

B

BACON, Jim (11) Leeds: 1920 - 1926.
BARENDS, David (2) Bradford: 1979.
BARTON, Frank (1) Wigan: 1951.
BARTON, John (2) Wigan: 1960 - 1961.
BASNETT, John (2) Widnes: 1984 - 1986.
BASSETT, Arthur (2) Halifax: 1946.
BATEMAN, Allan (1+2) Warrington: 1992 - 1994.
BATES, Alan (2+2) Dewsbury: 1974.
BATTEN, Billy (10) Hunslet & Hull: 1907 - 1921.
BATTEN, Eric (4) Bradford: 1946 - 1947.
BATTEN, Ray (3) Leeds: 1969 - 1973.
BAXTER, Johnnie (1) Rochdale Hornets: 1907.
BEAMES, Jack (2) Halifax: 1921.
BEARDMORE, Kevin (13+1) Castleford: 1984 - 1990.
BELSHAW, Billy (8) Liverpool St. & Warrington: 1936 - 1937.
BENNETT, Jack (7) Rochdale & Wigan: 1924 - 1926.
BENTHAM, Billy (2) Broughton Rangers: 1924.
BENTHAM, Nat (10) Wigan Highfield, Halifax and Warrington: 1928 - 1929.
BENTLEY, John (2) Leeds and Halifax: 1992 - 1994.
BENTLEY, Keith (1) Widnes: 1980.
BENYON, Billy (5+1) St.Helens: 1971 - 1972.
BETTS, Denis (30+2) Wigan & Auckland Warr.: 1990 - 1999.
BEVAN, Dai (1) Wigan: 1952.
BEVAN, John (6) Warrington: 1974 - 1978.
BEVERLEY, Harry (6) Hunslet & Halifax: 1936 - 1937.
BIBB, Chris (1) Featherstone Rovers: 1990.
BIRCH, Jim (1) Leeds: 1907.
BISHOP, David (+1) Hull K.R.: 1990.
BISHOP, Tommy (15) St.Helens: 1966 - 1969.
BLAN, Billy (3) Wigan: 1951.
BLINKHORN, Tom (1) Warrington: 1929.
BOLTON, David (23) Wigan: 1957 - 1963.
BOSTON, Billy (31) Wigan: 1954 - 1963.
BOTT, Charlie (1) Oldham: 1966.
BOWDEN, Jim (3) Huddersfield: 1954.
BOWEN, Frank (3) St.Helens Recs.: 1928.
BOWMAN, Eddie (4) Workington Town: 1977.
BOWMAN, Harold (8) Hull: 1924 - 1929.
BOWMAN, Ken (3) Huddersfield: 1962 - 1963.
BOYLEN, Frank (1) Hull: 1908.
BRADSHAW, Tommy (6) Wigan: 1947 - 1950.
BRIDGES, John "Keith" (3) Featherstone Rovers: 1974.
BRIERS, Lee (1) Warrington: 2001.
BRIGGS, Brian (1) Huddersfield: 1954

BROADBENT, Paul (8) Sheffield Eagles: 1996 - 1997.
BROGDEN, Stanley (16) Huddersfield & Leeds: 1929 - 1937.
BROOKE, Ian (13) Bradford & Wakefield: 1966 - 1968.
BROOKS, Ernest (3) Warrington: 1908.
BROUGH, Albert (2) Oldham: 1924.
BROUGH, Jim (5) Leeds: 1928 - 1936.
BROWN, Gordon (6) Leeds: 1954 - 1955.
BRYANT, Bill (4+1) Castleford: 1964 - 1967.
BUCKLEY, Alan (7) Swinton: 1963 - 1966.
BURGESS, Bill Snr. (16) Barrow: 1924 - 1929.
BURGESS, Bill Jnr. (14) Barrow: 1962 - 1969.
BURGHAM, Oliver (1) Halifax: 1911.
BURKE, Mick (14+1) Widnes: 1980 - 1986.
BURNELL, Alf (3) Hunslet: 1951 - 1954.
BURTON, Chris (8+1) Hull K.R.: 1982 - 1987.
BURWELL, Alan (7+1) Hull K.R.: 1967 - 1969.
BUTTERS, Fred (2) Swinton: 1929.

C

CAIRNS, David (2) Barrow: 1984.
CAMILLERI, Chris (2) Barrow: 1980.
CARLTON, Frank (2) St.Helens & Wigan: 1958 - 1962.
CARNEY, Brian (3) Wigan: 2003.
CARR, Charlie (7) Barrow: 1924 - 1926.
CARTWRIGHT, Joe (7) Leigh: 1920 - 1921.
CASE, Brian (6+1) Wigan: 1984 - 1988.
CASEY, Len (12+2) Hull K.R. & Bradford: 1977 - 1983.
CASSIDY, Mick (1+3) Wigan: 1994 - 1997.
CASTLE, Frank (4) Barrow: 1952 - 1954.
CHALLINOR, Jim (3) Warrington: 1958 - 1960.
CHARLTON, Paul (18+1) Workington & Salford: 1965 - 1974.
CHERRINGTON, Norman (1) Wigan: 1960.
CHILCOTT, Jack (3) **R.D.** (Huddersfield): 1914.
CHSINALL, David (2) Leigh: 1970.
CHISNALL, Eric (4) St.Helens: 1974.
CLAMPITT, James (3) Broughton Rangers: 1907 - 1914.
CLARK, Douglas (11) **R.D.** Huddersfield: 1911 - 1920.
CLARK, Garry (3) Hull K.R.: 1984 - 1985.
CLARK, Mick (5) Leeds: 1968.
CLARKE, Colin (7) Wigan: 1965 - 1973.
CLARKE, Phil (15+1) Wigan: 1990 - 1994.
CLAWSON, Terry (14) Featherstone Rovers, Leeds and Oldham: 1962 - 1974.
CLOSE, Don (1) Huddersfield: 1967.
COLDRICK, Percy (4) **R.D.** Wigan: 1914.
COLLIER, Frank (2) Wigan & Widnes: 1963 - 1964.
CONNOLLY, Gary (28+3) St.Helens, Wigan and Leeds: 1991 - 2003.
CORDLE, Gerald (1) Bradford: 1990.
COULMAN, Mike (2+1) Salford: 1971.
COURTNEY, Neil (+1) Warrington: 1982.
COVERDALE, Bob (4) Hull: 1954
COWIE, Neil (3) Wigan: 1993 - 1998.
CRACKNELL, Dick (2) Huddersfield: 1951.
CRANE, Mick (1) Hull: 1982.
CREASSER, David (2+2) Leeds: 1985 - 1988.
CROOKS, Lee (17+2) Hull, Leeds & Castleford: 1982 - 1994.
CROSTON, Jim (1) Castleford: 1937
CROWTHER, Hector (1) Hunslet: 1929.
CUMMINS, Francis (3) Leeds: 1998 - 1999.

CUNLIFFE, Billy (11) Warrington: 1920 - 1926.
CUNLIFFE, Jack (4) Wigan: 1950 - 1954.
CUNNIFFE, Bernard (1) Castleford: 1937.
CUNNINGHAM, Eddie (1) St.Helens: 1978.
CUNNINGHAM, Keiron (11) St.Helens: 1996 - 2002.
CURRAN, George (6) Salford: 1946 - 1948.
CURRIER, Andy (2) Widnes: 1989 - 1993.
CURZON, Ephraim (1) Salford: 1910.

D

DAGNALL, Bob (4) St.Helens: 1961 - 1965.
DALGREEN, John (1) Fulham: 1982.
DANBY, Tom (3) Salford: 1950.
DANIELS, Arthur (3) Halifax: 1952 - 1955.
DANNATT, Andy (3) Hull: 1985 - 1991.
DARWELL, Joe (5) Leigh: 1924.
DAVIES, Alan (20) Oldham: 1955 - 1960.
DAVIES, Billy (1) Swinton: 1968.
DAVIES, Billy J. (1) Castleford: 1933.
DAVIES, Evan (3) Oldham: 1920.
DAVIES, Jim (2) Huddersfield: 1911.
DAVIES, Jonathan (12+1) Widnes & Warrington: 1990 - 1994.
DAVIES, Will T. (1) Halifax: 1911.
DAVIES, William A. (2) **R.D.** Leeds: 1914.
DAVIES, Willie T.H. (3) Bradford: 1946 - 1947.
DAWSON, Edgar (1) York: 1956.
DEACON, Paul (7+1) Bradford: 2001 - 2003.
DERMOTT, Martin (11) Wigan: 1990 - 1993.
DEVEREUX, John (6+2) Widnes: 1992 - 1993.
DICK, Kevin (2) Leeds: 1980.
DICKENSON, George (1) Warrington: 1908.
DICKINSON, Roy (2) Leeds: 1985.
DINGSDALE, Billy (3) Warrington: 1929, 1933.
DIVORTY, Gary (2) Hull: 1985.
DIXON, Colin (12+2) Halifax & Salford: 1968 - 1974.
DIXON, Malcolm (2) Featherstone Rovers: 1962 - 1964.
DIXON, Paul (11+4) Halifax & Leeds: 1987 - 1992.
DOCKAR, Alec (1) Hull K.R.: 1947.
DONLAN, Steve (+2) Leigh: 1984.
DRAKE, Bill (1) Hull: 1962
DRAKE, Jim (1) Hull: 1960.
DRUMMOND, Des (24) Leigh & Warrington: 1980 - 1988.
DUANE, Ronnie (3) Warrington: 1983 - 1984.
DUTTON, Ray (6) Widnes: 1970.
DWYER, Bernard (+1) Bradford: 1996.
DYL, Les (11) Leeds: 1974 - 1982.
DYSON, Frank (1) Huddersfield: 1959.

E

EASTWOOD, Paul (13) Hull: 1990 - 1992.
ECCLES, Bob (1) Warrington: 1982.
ECCLES, Percy (1) Halifax: 1907.
ECKERSLEY, David (2+2) St.Helens: 1973 - 1974.
EDGAR, Brian (11) Workington Town: 1958 - 1966.
EDWARDS, Alan (7) Salford: 1936 - 1937.
EDWARDS, Derek (3+2) Castleford: 1968 - 1971.
EDWARDS, Shaun (32+4) Wigan: 1985 - 1994.
EGAN, Joe (14) Wigan: 1946 - 1950.
ELLABY, Alf (13) St.Helens: 1928 - 1933.
ELLIS, Gareth (+1) Wakefield Trinity: 2003.

ELLIS, Kevin (+1) Warrington: 1991.
ELLIS, St.John (+3) Castleford: 1991 - 1994.
ELWELL, Keith (3) Widnes: 1977 - 1980.
ENGLAND, Keith (6+5) Castleford: 1987 - 1991.
EVANS, Bryn (10) Swinton: 1926 - 1933.
EVANS, Frank (4) Swinton: 1924.
EVANS, Jack (4) Hunslet: 1951- 1952.
EVANS, Jack (3) Swinton: 1926.
EVANS, Roy (4) Wigan: 1961 - 1962.
EVANS, Steve (7+3) Featherstone & Hull: 1979 - 1982.
EYRE, Ken (1) Hunslet: 1965.
EYRES, Richard (3+6) Widnes: 1989 - 1993.

F

FAIRBAIRN, George (17) Wigan & Hull K.R.: 1977 - 1982.
FAIRBANK, Karl (10+6) Bradford: 1987 - 1994.
FAIRCLOUGH, Les (6) St.Helens: 1926 - 1929.
FARRAR, Vince (1) Hull: 1978.
FARRELL, Andrew (29) Wigan: 1993 - 2003.
FEATHERSTONE, Jimmy (6) Warrington: 1948 - 1952.
FEETHAM, Jack (8) Hull K.R. & Salford: 1929 - 1933.
FIELD, Harry (3) York: 1936.
FIELD, Norman (1) Batley: 1963.
FIELDEN, Stuart (8+3) Bradford: 2001 - 2003.
FIELDHOUSE, John (7) Widnes & St.Helens: 1985 - 1986.
FIELDING, Keith (3) Salford: 1974 - 1977.
FILDES, Alec (15) St.Helens Recs. & St.Helens: 1926 - 1932.
FISHER, Tony (11) Bradford & Leeds: 1970 - 1978.
FLANAGAN, Peter (14) Hull K.R.: 1962 - 1970.
FLANAGAN, Terry (4) Oldham: 1983 - 1984.
FLEARY, Darren (1+1) Leeds: 1998.
FOGERTY, Terry (2+1) Halifax, Wigan & RochdaleHornets: 1966 - 1974.
FORD, Michael (+2) Castleford: 1993.
FORD, Phil (13) Wigan, Bradford & Leeds: 1985 - 1989.
FORSHAW, Mike (8+6) Bradford: 1997 - 2003.
FORSTER, Mark (2) Warrington: 1987.
FOSTER, Frank (1) Hull K.R.: 1967.
FOSTER, Peter (3) Leigh: 1955.
FOSTER, Trevor (3) Bradford: 1946 - 1948.
FOX, Deryck (10+4) Featherstone & Bradford: 1985 - 1992.
FOX, Don (1) Featherstone Rovers: 1963.
FOX, Neil (29) Wakefield Trinity: 1959 - 1969.
FOY, Des (3) Oldham: 1984 - 1985.
FRANCIS, Bill (4) Wigan: 1967 - 1977.
FRANCIS, Roy (1) Barrow: 1947.
FRASER, Eric (16) Warrington: 1958 - 1961.
FRENCH, Ray (4) Widnes: 1968.
FRODSHAM, Alf (3) St.Helens: 1928 - 1929.

G

GABBITAS, Brian (1) Hunslet: 1959.
GALLAGHER, Frank (12) Dewsbury & Batley: 1920 - 1926.
GANLEY, Bernard (3) Oldham: 1957 - 1958.
GARDINER, Danny (1) Wigan: 1965.
GEE, Ken (17) Wigan: 1946 - 1951.
GEMMELL, Dick (3) Leeds & Hull: 1964 - 1969.
GIBSON, Carl (10+1) Batley & Leeds: 1985 - 1991.
GIFFORD, Harry (2) Barrow: 1908.
GILFEDDER, Laurie (5) Warrington: 1962 - 1963.

GILL, Henderson (14+1) Wigan: 1981 - 1988.
GILL, Ken (5+2) Salford: 1974 - 1977.
GILMOUR, Lee (4+3) Wigan, Bradford & St.Helens: 1998 - 2003
GLEESON, Martin (4+1) St.Helens: 2002 - 2003.
GOODWAY, Andy (23) Oldham & Wigan: 1983 - 1990.
GOODWIN, Dennis (5) Barrow: 1957 - 1958.
GORE, Jack (1) Salford: 1926.
GORLEY, Les (4+1) Widnes: 1980 -1982.
GORLEY, Peter (2+1) St.Helens: 1980 - 1981.
GOULDING, Bobbie (13+2) Wigan, Leeds & St.Helens: 1990 - 1997.
GOWERS, Ken (14) Swinton: 1962 - 1966.
GRAY, John (5+3) Wigan: 1974.
GRAYSHON, Jeff (13) Bradford & Leeds: 1979 - 1985.
GREENALL, Doug (6) St.Helens: 1951 - 1954.
GREENALL, Johnny (1) St.Helens Recs.: 1921.
GREENHOUGH, Bobby (1) Warrington: 1960.
GREGORY, Andy (25+1) Widnes, Warrington & Wigan: 1981 - 1992.
GREGORY, Mike (19+1) Warrington: 1987 - 1990.
GRIBBIN, Vince (1) Whitehaven: 1985.
GRIFFITHS, Jonathan (1) St.Helens (1992).
GRONOW, Ben (7) Huddersfield: 1911 - 1920.
GROVES, Paul (1) St.Helens: 1987.
GRUNDY, Jack (12) Barrow: 1955 - 1957.
GUNNEY, Geoff (11) Hunslet: 1954 - 1965.
GWYNNE, Emlyn (3) Hull: 1929 - 1929.
GWYTHER, Elwyn (6) Belle Vue Rangers: 1947 - 1951.

H

HAGGERTY, Roy (2) St.Helens: 1987.
HAIGH, Bob (5+1) Wakefield & Leeds: 1968 - 1971.
HALL, Billy (4) **R.D.** Oldham: 1914.
HALL, David (2) Hull K.R.: 1984.
HALLAS, Derek (2) Leeds: 1961.
HALMSHAW, Tony (1) Halifax: 1971.
HALSALL, Hector (1) Swinton: 1929.
HAMMOND, Karle (1+1) St.Helens: 1996.
HAMPSON, Steve (11+1) Wigan: 1987 - 1992.
HANLEY, Ellery (35+1) Bradford, Wigan & Leeds: 1984 - 1993.
HARDISTY, Alan (12) Castleford: 1964 - 1970.
HARE, Ian (1) Widnes: 1967.
HARKIN, Paul (+1) Hull K.R.: 1985.
HARRIS, Iestyn (7+2) Warrington & Leeds: 1996 - 1999.
HARRIS, Tommy (25) Hull: 1954 - 1960.
HARRISON, Fred (3) Leeds: 1911.
HARRISON, Karl (11+5) Hull & Halifax: 1990 - 1994.
HARRISON, Mick (7) Hull: 1967 - 1973.
HARTLEY, Dennis (11) Hunslet & Castleford: 1964 - 1970.
HARTLEY, Steve (3) Hull K.R.: 1980 - 1981.
HAUGHTON, Simon (+5) Wigan: 1997 - 1998.
HAY, Andy (+2) Leeds: 1999.
HAYES, Joey (1) St.Helens: 1996.
HELME, Gerry (12) Warrington: 1948 - 1954.
HEPWORTH, Keith (11) Castleford: 1967 - 1970.
HERBERT, Norman (6) Workington Town: 1961 - 1962.
HERON, David (1+1) Leeds: 1982.
HESKETH, Chris (21+2) Salford: 1970 - 1974.

HICKS, Mervyn (1) St.Helens: 1965.
HIGGINS, Fred (6) Widnes: 1950 - 1951.
HIGGINS, Harold (2) Widnes: 1937.
HIGSON, John (2) Hunslet: 1908.
HILL, Cliff (1) Wigan: 1966.
HILL, David (1) Wigan: 1971.
HILTON, Herman (7) Oldham: 1920 - 1921.
HILTON, Jack (4) Wigan: 1950.
HOBBS, David (10+2) Featherstone, Oldham & Bradford: 1984 - 1989.
HODGSON, David (1+1) Wigan: 2001.
HODGSON, Martin (16) Swinton: 1929 - 1937.
HOGAN, Phil (6+3) Barrow & Hull K.R.: 1977 - 1979.
HOGG, Andrew (1) Broughton Rangers: 1907.
HOLDEN, Keith (1) Warrington: 1963.
HOLDER, Billy (1) Hull: 1907.
HOLDING, Neil (4) St.Helens: 1984.
HOLDSTOCK, Roy (2) Hull K.R.: 1980.
HOLLAND, David (4) **R.D.** Oldham: 1914.
HOLLIDAY, Bill (9+1) Whitehaven & Hull K.R.: 1964 - 1967.
HOLLIDAY, Les (3) Widnes: 1991 - 1992.
HOLLINDRAKE, Terry (1) Keighley: 1955.
HOLMES, John (14+6) Leeds: 1971 - 1982.
HORNE, Richard (3+5) Hull: 2001 - 2003.
HORNE, Willie (8) Barrow: 1946 - 1952.
HORTON, Bill (14) Wakefield Trinity: 1928 - 1933.
HOWARD, Harvey (+1) Bradford: 1998.
HUDDART, Dick (16) Whitehaven & St.Helens: 1958 - 1963.
HUDSON, Barney (8) Salford: 1932 - 1937.
HUDSON, Bill (1) Wigan: 1948.
HUGHES, Eric (8) Widnes: 1978 - 1982.
HULME, David (7+1) Widnes: 1988 - 1989.
HULME, Paul (3+5) Widnes: 1988 - 1992.
HUNTE, Alan (15) St.Helens: 1992 - 1997.
HURCOMBE, Danny (8) Wigan: 1920 - 1924.
HYNES, Syd (12+1) Leeds: 1970 -1973.

I

IRVING, Bob (8+3) Oldham: 1967 - 1972.
IRWIN, Shaun (+4) Castleford: 1990.

J

JACKSON, Ken (2) Oldham: 1957.
JACKSON, Lee (17) Hull & Sheffield Eagles : 1990 - 1994.
JACKSON, Michael (2+4) Wakefield & Halifax: 1991 - 1993.
JACKSON, Phil (27) Barrow: 1954 - 1958.
JAMES, Neil (1) Halifax: 1986.
JARMAN, Billy (2) Leeds: 1914.
JASIEWICZ, Dick (1) Bradford: 1984.
JEANES, David (8) Wakefield & Leeds: 1971 - 1972.
JENKINS, Bert (12) Wigan: 1907 - 1914.
JENKINS, Dai (1) Hunslet: 1929.
JENKINS, Dai (1) Hunslet: 1947.
JENKINS, Emlyn (9) Salford: 1933 - 1937.
JENKINSON, Albert (2) Hunslet: 1911.
JOHNSON, Albert (4) **R.D.** Widnes: 1914 - 1920.
JOHNSON, Albert (6) Warrington: 1946 - 1947.
JOHNSON, Chris (1) Leigh: 1985.
JOHNSON, Paul (5) Wigan: 2001 - 2002.
JOLLEY, Jim (3) Runcorn: 1907

JONES, Berwyn (3) Wakefield Trinity: 1964 - 1966.
JONES, Dai (2) Merthyr: 1907.
JONES, Ernest (4) Rochdale Hornets: 1920.
JONES, Joe (1) Barrow: 1946.
JONES, Keri (2) Wigan: 1970.
JONES, Les (1) St.Helens: 1971.
JONES, Lewis (15) Leeds: 1954 - 1957.
JONES, Mark (+1) Hull: 1992.
JORDAN, Gary (2) Featherstone Rovers: 1964 - 1967.
JOYNER, John (14+2) Castleford: 1978 - 1984.
JOYNT, Chris (19+6) St.Helens: 1993 - 2002.
JUBB, Ken (2) Leeds: 1937.
JUKES, Bill (6) Hunslet: 1908 - 1910.

K

KARALIUS, Tony (4+1) St.Helens: 1971 - 1972.
KARALIUS, Vince (12) St.Helens & Widnes: 1958 - 1963.
KEEGAN, Arthur (9) Hull: 1966 - 1969.
KELLY, Ken (4) St.Helens & Warrington: 1972 - 1982.
KEMEL, George (2) Widnes: 1965.
KERSHAW, Herbert (2) Wakefield Trinity: 1910.
KING, Paul (1) Hull: 2001.
KINNEAR, Roy (1) Wigan: 1929.
KISS, Nicky (1) Wigan: 1985.
KITCHEN, Frank (2) Leigh: 1954.
KITCHIN, Philip (1) Whitehaven: 1965.
KITCHING, Jack (1) Bradford: 1946.
KNAPMAN, Ernest (1) Oldham: 1924.
KNOWELDEN, Bryn (1) Barrow: 1946.

L

LAUGHTON, Dale (4+1) Sheffield Eagles: 1998 - 1999.
LAUGHTON, Doug (15) Wigan & Widnes: 1970 - 1979.
LAWRENSON, John ny (3) Wigan: 1948.
LAWS, David (1) Hull K.R.: 1986.
LEDGARD, Jim (11) Dewsbury & Leigh: 1947 - 1954.
LEDGER, Barry (2) St.Helens: 1985 - 1986.
LEWIS, Gordon (1) Leigh: 1965.
LEYTHAM, Jim (5) Wigan: 1907 - 1910.
LITTLE, Syd (10) Oldham: 1956 - 1958.
LLEWELLYN, Tom (2) Oldham: 1907.
LLOYD, Robbie (1) Halifax: 1920.
LOCKWOOD, Brian (8+1) Castleford & Hull K.R.:
1972 - 1979.
LOMAS, Jim (7) Salford & Oldham: 1908 - 1911.
LONG, Sean (2+5) St.Helens: 1997 - 2003.
LONGSTAFF, Fred (2) Huddersfield: 1914.
LONGWORTH, Bill (3) Oldham: 1908.
LOUGHLIN, Paul (14+1) St.Helens: 1988 - 1992.
LOWE, John (1) Leeds: 1932.
LOWE, Phil (12) Hull K.R.: 1970 - 1978.
LOWES, James (5) Bradford: 1997 - 2002.
LOXTON, Ken (1) Huddersfield: 1971.
LUCAS, Ian (1+1) Wigan: 1991 - 1992.
LYDON, Joe (23+7) Widnes & Wigan: 1983 - 1992.

M

McCORMICK, Stan (3) Belle Vue Rangers & St.Helens: 1948.
McCUE, Tommy (6) Widnes: 1936 - 1946.
McCURRIE, Steve (1) Widnes: 1993.

McDERMOTT, Barrie (11+3) Wigan & Leeds: 1994 - 2003.
McDERMOTT, Brian (4) Bradford: 1996 - 1997.
McGINTY, Billy (4) Wigan: 1992.
McINTYRE, Len (1) Oldham: 1963.
McKEATING, Vince (2) Workington Town: 1951.
McKINNEY, Tom (11) Salford, Warrington & St.Helens:
1951 - 1957.
McNAMARA, Steve (+4) Hull & Bradford: 1992 - 1997.
McTIGUE, Brian (25) Wigan: 1958 - 1963.
MANN, Arthur (2) Bradford: 1908.
MANTLE, John (13) St.Helens: 1966 - 1973.
MARCHANT, Tony (3) Castleford: 1986.
MARTIN, Bill (1) Workington Town: 1962.
MARTYN, Mick (2) Leigh: 1958 -1959.
MATHER, Barrie-Jon (1+2) Wigan & Perth Reds: 1994 - 1996.
MATHIAS, Roy (1) St.Helens: 1979.
MEASURES, Jim (2) Widnes: 1963.
MEDLEY, Paul (3+1) Leeds: 1987 - 1988.
MIDDLETON, Alf (1) Salford: 1929.
MILLER, Joe (1) Wigan: 1911.
MILLER, Joe "Jack" (6) Warrington: 1933 -1936.
MILLS, Jim (6) Widnes: 1974 - 1979.
MILLWARD, Roger (28+1) Castleford & Hull K.R.:
1966 - 1978.
MILNES, Alf (2) Halifax: 1920.
MOLLOY, Steve (2+2) Leeds & Featherstone: 1993 - 1996.
MOONEY, Walter (2) Leigh: 1924.
MOORHOUSE, Stanley (2) Huddersfield: 1914.
MORGAN, Arnold (4) Featherstone Rovers: 1968.
MORGAN, Edgar (2) Hull: 1921.
MORGAN, Ron (2) Swinton: 1963.
MORIARTY, Paul (1+1) Widnes: 1991 - 1994.
MORLEY, Adrian (9+3) Leeds & Sydney Roosters: 1996- 2003.
MORLEY, Jack (2) Wigan: 1936 - 1937.
MOSES, Glyn (9) St.Helens: 1955 - 1957.
MUMBY, Keith (11) Bradford: 1982 - 1984.
MURPHY, Alex (27) St.Helens & Warrington: 1958 - 1971.
MURPHY, Harry (1) Wakefield Trinity: 1950.
MYLER, Frank (23+1) Widnes & St.Helens: 1960 - 1970.
MYLER, Tony (14) Widnes: 1983 - 1986.

N

NASH, Steve (24) Featherstone & Salford: 1971 - 1982.
NAUGHTON, Albert (2) Warrington: 1954.
NEWBOULD, Tommy (1) Wakefield Trinity: 1910.
NEWLOVE, Paul (16+4) Featherstone, Bradford & St.Helens:
1989 - 1998.
NEWTON, Terry (4+1) Leeds & Wigan: 1998 - 2003.
NICHOLLS, George (29) Widnes & St.Helens: 1971 - 1979.
NICHOLSON, Bob (3) Huddersfield: 1946 - 1948.
NICKLE, Sonny (1+5) St.Helens: 1992 -1994.
NOBLE, Brian (11) Bradford: 1982 - 1984.
NORTON, Steve (11+1) Castleford & Hull: 1974 - 1982.
O'CONNOR, Terry (11+2) Wigan: 1996 - 2002.

O

OFFIAH, Martin (33) Widnes & Wigan: 1988 - 1994.
O'GRADY,Terry (6) Oldham & Warrington: 1954 -1961.
OLIVER, Joe (4) Batley: 1928.

O'NEILL, Dennis (2+1) Widnes: 1971 - 1972.
O'NEILL, Mike (3) Widnes: 1982 -1983.
ORR, Danny (+2) Castleford: 2002.
OSTER, Jack (1) Oldham: 1929.
OWEN, Jim (1) St.Helens Recs.: 1921.
OWEN, Stan (1) Leigh: 1958.
OWENS, Ike (4) Leeds: 1946.

P

PADBURY, Dick (1) Runcorn: 1908.
PALIN, Harold (2) Warrington: 1947.
PARKER, Dave (2) Oldham: 1964.
PARKER, Jonathan (17) Wakefield Trinity: 1920 - 1929.
PARR, Ken (1) Warrington: 1968.
PAWSEY, Charlie (7) Leigh: 1952 - 1954.
PEACOCK, Jamie (7+3) Bradford: 2001 - 2003.
PEPPERELL, Albert (2) Workington Town: 1950 -1951.
PHILLIPS, Doug (4) Oldham & Belle Vue R.: 1946 - 1950.
PHILLIPS, Rowland (+1) Workington Town: 1996.
PIMBLETT, Albert (3) Warrington: 1948.
PINNER, Harry (6+1) St.Helens: 1980 -1986.
PITCHFORD, Frank (2) Oldham: 1958 -1962.
PITCHFORD, Steve (4) Leeds: 1977.
PLANGE, David (1) Castleford: 1988.
PLATT, Andy (21+4) St.Helens & Wigan: 1985 - 1993.
POLLARD, Charlie (1) Wakefield Trinity: 1924.
POLLARD, Ernest (2) Wakefield Trinity: 1932.
POLLARD, Roy (1) Dewsbury: 1950.
POOLE, Harry (3) Hull K.R.: 1964 - 1966.
POTTER, Ian (7+1) Wigan: 1985 - 1986.
POWELL, Daryl (23+10) Sheffield & Keighley: 1990 - 1996.
POWELL, Roy (13+6) Leeds: 1985 - 1991.
POYNTON, Harold (3) Wakefield Trinity: 1962.
PRATT, Karl (2) Leeds: 2002.
PRESCOTT, Alan (28) St.Helens: 1951 - 1958.
PRICE, Gary H. (+1) Wakefield Trinity: 1991.
PRICE, Jack (6) Broughton Rangers & Wigan: 1921 - 1924.
PRICE, Malcolm (2) Rochdale Hornets: 1967.
PRICE, Ray (9) Warrington: 1954 - 1957.
PRICE, Terry (1) Bradford: 1970.
PRIOR, Bernard (1) Hunslet: 1966.
PROCTOR, Wayne (+1) Hull: 1984.
PROSSER, Dai (1) Leeds: 1937.
PROSSER, Stuart (1) **R.D.** Halifax: 1914.
PRYCE, Leon (6) Bradford: 2001 - 2002.

R

RADLINSKI, Kris (20) Wigan: 1996 - 2003.
RAE, Johnny (1) Bradford: 1965.
RAMSDALE, Dick (8) **R.D.** Wigan: 1910 - 1914.
RAMSEY, Bill (7+1) Hunslet & Bradford: 1965 - 1974.
RATCLIFFE, Gordon (3) Wigan: 1947- 1950.
RATHBONE, Alan (4+1) Bradford: 1982 - 1985.
RAYNE, Keith (4) Leeds: 1984.
RAYNE, Kevin (1) Leeds: 1986.
REDFEARN, Alan (1) Bradford: 1979.
REDFEARN, David (6+1) Bradford: 1972 - 1974.
REES, Billo (11) Swinton: 1926 - 1929.
REES, Dai (1) Halifax: 1926.
REES, Tom (1) Oldham: 1929.

REILLY, Malcolm (9) Castleford: 1970.
RENILSON, Charlie (7+1) Halifax: 1965 - 1968.
RHODES, Austin (4) St.Helens: 1957 - 1961.
RICHARDS, Maurice (2) Salford: 1974.
RILEY, Joe (1) Halifax: 1910.
RING, Johnny (2) Wigan: 1924- 1926.
RISMAN, Bev (5) Leeds: 1968.
RISMAN, Gus (17) Salford: 1932 - 1946.
RIX, Sid (9) Oldham: 1924 -1926.
ROBERTS, Ken (10) Halifax: 1963 - 1966.
ROBINSON, Asa (3) Halifax: 1907 -1908.
ROBINSON, Dave (13) Swinton & Wigan: 1965 - 1970.
ROBINSON, Bill (2) Leigh: 1963.
ROBINSON, Don (10) Wakefield & Leeds: 1954 - 1960.
ROBINSON, Jack (2) Rochdale Hornets: 1914.
ROBINSON, Jason (12) Wigan: 1993 - 1999.
ROGERS, Johnny (7) Huddersfield 1914 - 1921.
ROSE, David (4) Leeds: 1954.
ROSE, Paul (2+3) Hull K.R. & Hull: 1974 - 1982.
ROUND, Gerry (8) Wakefield Trinity: 1959 - 1962.
RUDDICK, George (3) Broughton Rangers: 1907 - 1910.
RYAN, Bob (5) Warrington: 1950 - 1952.
RYAN, Martin (4) Wigan: 1947 - 1950.
RYDER, Ron (1) Warrington: 1952.

S

SAMPSON, Dean (+1) Castleford: 1997.
SAYER, Bill (7) Wigan: 1961 - 1963.
SCHOFIELD, Derrick (1) Halifax: 1955.
SCHOFIELD, Garry (44-2) Hull & Leeds: 1984 - 1994.
SCULTHORPE, Paul (19+2) Warrington & St.Helens: 1996 - 2003.
SEABOURNE, Barry (1) Leeds: 1970.
SENIOR, Keith (14+2) Sheffield Eagles & Leeds: 1996 - 2003.
SENIOR, Ken (2) Huddersfield: 1965 - 1967.
SHARROCK, Jim (4) Wigan: 1910 - 1911.
SHAW, Brian (5) Hunslet & Leeds: 1956 - 1961.
SHAW, Glyn (1) Widnes: 1980.
SHAW, John "Joby" (5) Halifax: 1960 - 1962.
SHELTON, Geoff (7) Hunslet: 1964 - 1966.
SHERIDAN, Ryan (3) Leeds: 1999 - 2002.
SHOEBOTTOM, Mick (10+2) Leeds: 1968 - 1971.
SHUGARS, Frank (1) Warrington: 1910.
SILCOCK, Dick (1) Wigan: 1908.
SILCOCK, Nat Snr. (12) Widnes: 1932 - 1937.
SILCOCK, Nat Jnr. (3) Wigan: 1954.
SIMMS, Barry (1) Leeds: 1962.
SINFIELD, Kevin (4+5) Leeds: 2001 - 2003.
SKELHORNE, George "Jack" (7) Warrington: 1920 - 1921.
SKERRETT, Kelvin (14+2) Bradford & Wigan: 1989 - 1993.
SKERRETT, Trevor (10) Wakefield & Hull: 1979 - 1982.
SLOMAN, Bob (3) Oldham: 1928.
SMALES, Tommy (8) Huddersfield & Bradford: 1962 - 1965.
SMALL, Peter (1) Castleford: 1962.
SMITH, Alan (10) Leeds: 1970 - 1973.
SMITH, Arthur (6) Oldham: 1907 - 1908.
SMITH, Bert (2) Bradford: 1926.
SMITH, Fred (9) **R.D.** Hunslet: 1910 -1914.
SMITH, Geoff (3) York: 1963 - 1964.
SMITH, Mike (10+1) Hull K.R.: 1979 - 1984.

SMITH, Peter (1+5) Featherstone Rovers: 1977 - 1984.
SMITH, Sam (4) Hunslet: 1954.
SMITH, Stanley (11) Wakefield Trinity: 1929 - 1933.
SMITH, Tony (3+2) Castleford & Wigan: 1996 - 1998.
SOUTHWARD, Ike (11) Workington & Oldham: 1958 - 1962.
SPENCER, Jack (1) Salford: 1907.
SPRUCE, Stuart (6) Widnes & Bradford: 1993 - 1996.
STACEY, Cyril (1) Hunslet: 1920.
STEADMAN, Graham (9+1) Castleford: 1990 -1994.
STEPHENS, Gary (5) Castleford: 1979.
STEPHENSON, David (9+1) Wigan & Leeds: 1982 - 1988.
STEPHENSON, Mike (5+1) Dewsbury: 1971 - 1972.
STEVENSON, Jeff (19) Leeds & York: 1955 - 1960.
STOCKWELL, Squire (3) Leeds: 1920 -1921.
STONE, Billy (8) Hull: 1920 -1921.
STOPFORD, John (12) Swinton: 1961 - 1966.
STOTT, Jim (1) St.Helens: 1947.
STREET, Harry (4) Dewsbury: 1950.
SULLIVAN, Anthony (7) St.Helens: 1991 - 1999.
SULLIVAN, Clive (17) Hull: 1967 - 1973.
SULLIVAN, Jim (25) Wigan: 1924 - 1933.
SULLIVAN, Mick (46) Huddersfield, Wigan, St.Helens & York: 1954 - 1963.
SZYMALA, Eddie (1+1) Barrow: 1981.

T

TAIT, Alan (10+4) Widnes & Leeds: 1989 - 1993.
TAYLOR, Bob (2) Hull: 1921 -1926.
TAYLOR, Harry (3) Hull: 1907.
TEMBEY, John (2) St.Helens: 1963 - 1964.
TERRY, Abe (11) St.Helens & Leeds: 1958 - 1962.
THOMAS, Arthur "Ginger" (4) Leeds: 1926 - 1929.
THOMAS, George (1) Warrington: 1907.
THOMAS, Gwyn (9) Wigan & Huddersfield: 1914 - 1921.
THOMAS, Johnny (8) Wigan: 1907 - 1911.
THOMAS, Les (1) Oldham: 1947.
THOMAS, Phil (1) Leeds: 1907.
THOMPSON, Cec (2) Hunslet: 1951.
THOMPSON, Jimmy (20+1) Featherstone & Bradford: 1970 - 1978.
THOMPSON, Joe (12) Leeds: 1924 - 1932.
THORLEY, John (4) Halifax: 1954.
TOOHEY, Ted (3) Barrow: 1952.
TOPLISS, David (4) Wakefield Trinity & Hull: 1973 - 1982.
TRAILL, Ken (8) Bradford: 1950 - 1954.
TROUP, Alec (2) Barrow: 1936.
TURNBULL, Drew (1) Leeds: 1951.
TURNER, Derek (24) Oldham & Wakefield: 1956 - 1962.
TYSON, Brian (3) Hull K.R.: 1963 - 1967.

V

VALENTINE, Dave (15) Huddersfield: 1948 - 1954.
VALENTINE, Rob (1) Huddersfield: 1967.
VINES, Don (3) Wakefield Trinity: 1959.

W

WADDELL, Hugh (5) Oldham & Leeds: 1988 - 1989.
WAGSTAFF, Harold (12) **R.D.** Huddersfield: 1911 - 1921.
WALKER, Aronold (1) Whitehaven: 1980.
WALLACE, Jim (1) St.Helens Recs.: 1926.
WALSH, Joe (1) Leigh: 1971.
WALSH, John (4+1) St.Helens: 1972.

Harry Pinner and Ellery Hanley pictured after a Great Britain Test win over New Zealand in 1985.

WALTON, Doug (1) Castleford: 1965.
WANE, Shaun (2) Wigan: 1985 - 1986.
WARD, Billy (1) Leeds: 1910.
WARD, David (12) Leeds: 1977 - 1982.
WARD, Ernest (20) Bradford: 1946 - 1952.
WARD, Johnny (4) Castleford & Salford: 1963 - 1970.
WARD, Kevin (15+2) Castleford & St.Helens: 1984 - 1992.
WARD, Ted (3) Wigan: 1946 - 1947.
WARLOW, John (6+1) St.Helens & Widnes: 1964 - 1971.
WARWICK, Silas (2) Salford: 1907.
WATKINS, Billy (7) Salford: 1933 - 1937.
WATKINS, David (2+4) Salford: 1971 - 1974.
WATKINSON, David (12+1) Hull K.R.: 1979 - 1986.
WATSON, Cliff (29+1) St.Helens: 1963 - 1971.
WATTS, Basil (5) York: 1954 - 1955.
WEBSTER, Fred (3) Leeds: 1910.
WELLENS, Paul (3+2) St.Helens: 2001 - 2002.
WHITCOMBE, Frank (2) Bradford: 1946.
WHITE, Les (7) Hunslet: 1932 - 1933.
WHITE, Les (6) York & Wigan: 1946 - 1947.
WHITE, Tommy (3) Oldham: 1907.
WHITEHEAD, Derek (3) Warrington: 1971.
WHITELEY, Johnny (15) 1957 - 1962.
WILKINSON, Jack (11) Halifax & Wakefield: 1954 - 1962.
WILLIAMS, Billy (2) Salford: 1929 - 1932.
WILLIAMS, Dickie (12) Leeds & Hunslet: 1948 - 1954.
WILLIAMS, Frank (2) **R.D.** Halifax: 1914.
WILLIAMS, Peter (1+1) Salford: 1989.
WILLICOMBE, David (3) Halifax & Wigan: 1974.
WOOD, Alf (4) **R.D.** Oldham: 1911 - 1914.
WOODS, Harry (6) Liverpool Stanley & Leeds: 1936 - 1937.
WOODS, Jack (1) Barrow: 1933.
WOODS, John (7+4) Leigh & Warrington: 1979 - 1987.
WOODS, Tommy (2) Rochdale Hornets: 1911.
WORRALL, Mick (3) Oldham: 1984.
WRIGHT, Darren (+1) Widnes, 1988.
WRIGHT, Joe (1) Swinton: 1932.
WRIGHT, Stuart (7) Widnes: 1977 - 1978.
WRIGLESWORTH, Geoff (5) Leeds: 1965 - 1966.

Y

YOUNG, Chris (5) Hull K.R.: 1967 - 1968.
YOUNG, Frank (1) Leeds: 1908.
YOUNG, Harold (1) Huddersfield: 1929.

The FINAL WHISTLE

When "Rugby League Journal" was launched in December 2002 our aim was two-fold. Firstly, to enjoy wallowing in nostalgia by sharing our memories and a large collection of memorabilia and photographs ammassed over the years; secondly, to provide a reassuring voice in the media for the silent majority of old fashioned Rugby League followers who had seen the game and so many things surrounding it change almost beyond recognition from the world they were brought up in.

It has been very satisfying to learn that "Rugby League Journal" brings so much pleasure to so many people who enjoy looking back on the players, teams and events they remember from younger days, and at the same time to know we are helping new generations to learn more about the great history and folklore of Rugby League.

This book, our first "Rugby League Journal Annual" came about because with just four issues per year of the "Journal" we felt we wanted to give more to those fans "who don't want to forget." There was much more memorabilia and more old photographs to share with you and we hope this bumper package of the "Annual" will provide much enjoyment for Rugby League fans as the year 2004 turns into 2005. We also hope it will encourage you to subscribe to the "Journal" and enjoy our coverage on a regular basis throughout the year.

My passion for the international game continues and in the modern game there remains nothing better than full bloodied Test matches between Great Britain, Australia and New Zealand. Those of us who can remember when France was also up there with the major Rugby League nations hope we live to see those days return - which makes it all the more important we preserve the memories of what has gone before. With that in mind, I hope this "Annual" will be just the first of many more books from Rugby League Journal Publishing.

2004 has been a vastly entertaining year in Rugby League. Congratulations should go to the high achievers: to Leeds and Bradford for making the Grand Final, to St.Helens the Challenge Cup winners, to Leigh and Whitehaven, to Barrow and to the Coventry Bears (the latter perhaps a pointer of things to come in the expanding world of Rugby League), and in the Amateur game to Wath Brow Hornets and Siddal. At so many different levels, your efforts and skills make the game what it is.

Happy reading.
The Editor

Additional copies of this Annual can be obtained by post from the address below, price £11.95 per book plus £2.00 postage and packing per book. Please pay by cheque/postal order made payable to "Rugby League Journal."

RUGBY LEAGUE JOURNAL
PUBLISHING

P.O. Box 22, Egremont, Cumbria, CA23 3WA
E-mail: rugbyleague.journal@virgin.net   Telephone: 01946 814249
www.rugbyleaguejournal.com